D1525792

Floridians

Real Stories from the Sunshine State

Ronald W. Kenyon

The Poinciana Press

2016

Floridians: Real Stories from the Sunshine State is a work of non-fiction. While the incidents related herein did occur, some of the names and personal characteristics of the individuals cited herein have been changed to protect their identities.

The author has striven for accuracy and has endeavored to verify all factual information. All the opinions expressed herein are the author's, and he alone bears the responsibility for any errors in the text.

Photographs by the author except where indicated.

Picture credits:

Front cover: Lake County (IL) Discovery Museum, Curt Teich Postcard Archives; Page 15, Sidelines. Inc.; Page 22, SMasters, Wikimedia Commons; Page 54, Alchetron.com; Page 67, Nikater, Wikimedia Commons; Page 79, RealClearPolitics; Page 113 The Cornucopia Institute; Page 123, Editions Stock, Amazon.com; Page 146, Florida Department of Corrections; Page 157, Wikimedia Commons.

This book is available at quantity discounts for bulk purchase. For information, please email the author at rwkenyon@gmail.com.

First Edition

ISBN-13: 978-1530907908
ISBN-10: 153090790X

I am now in the hot gardens of the sun, where the palm meets the pine.

--John Muir, *A Thousand-Mile Walk to the Gulf*

Florida provides a true mirror of what America is becoming—what it already is, in fact.

--T. D. Allman, *Finding Florida*

Contents

Introduction

When I was young back in the 1950s, every summer vacation my father would drive my mother, my younger brother and me from our home in Kentucky to a different part of Florida. My parents' goal was to find a place to retire. My brother and I were just along for the ride.

Over nearly a decade, we explored places from one end of the state to the other. We played in the quiet surf and the pristine, sugary sands of Santa Rosa Island on the Panhandle and scavenged for petrified megalodon sharks' teeth on the beach at Venice. In Saint Augustine, we explored the Castillo de San Marcos, the fortress built by the Spanish in the late seventeenth century. I'll never forget Hobe Sound, where we saw paved streets equipped with lampposts and sewers but not a single dwelling, the stillborn embryo of a town named Picture City, intended to be a motion picture production center, a victim of the 1928 hurricane and the Great Depression.

We bought recordings of Latin American music and saw the jai alai fronton in Tampa's Ybor City. One year, we followed the Withlacoochie River, passing through neighboring communities with the improbable names of Yankeetown and Crackertown and traveled to the secluded fishing village of Cedar Key, where naturalist and preservationist John Muir arrived on October 23, 1867, after a thousand-mile walk from Louisville, Kentucky.

We laughed at the antics of the boat-tailed grackles squabbling in the palmettos. And we played lots of shuffleboard.

One year, after visiting Miami (the only thing I remember was Vizcaya, industrialist James Deering's Italian renaissance villa and gardens on Biscayne Bay), we drove all the way to Key West. Once there, my father refused my pleas to board a sailing vessel and venture 90 miles further into the Gulf of Mexico to Fort Jefferson in the Dry Tortugas, where Dr. Samuel Mudd, convicted for his involvement in the plot to assassinate President Lincoln, had ministered to the prisoners taken ill with yellow fever in 1867. In retrospect, I realize that I saw more of Florida on those vacations than most Floridians see today.

I have been writing essays all my life, so I couldn't resist writing about the Sunshine State after moving here after having lived for a decade in Paris. The result is this book, the third in a series of Real Stories, the others being collections written while I was living in France and on the island kingdom of Bahrain.

The cast of characters in these seventeen stories of fascinating Floridians includes the living and the dead, the famous and the infamous—murderers, imposters, royal pretenders, a supermarket cashier, a housekeeper, a homeless former crack addict rescued by an anonymous benefactor, the woman who was elected chief of the Seminoles, a Jordanian Cordon Bleu chef, a chess champion who founded a city and the first two Jewish senators. Even John Lennon makes an appearance.

2

Many of the essays in this book are excursions from the personal to the universal, from microcosm to macrocosm. For example, a search for fresh eggs leads to a denunciation of the $45 billion poultry industry and the discovery that chickens are omnivorous. A search for a sportscoat leads to the human trafficking of Asian wage-slaves on the island of Saipan and a prestigious American clothier that succumbed to changing fashions.

Other chapters begin with the banal and end with a quirky or unexpected surprise; thus a trip to the supermarket ends in a discussion of racism and a marriage proposal, and a chance encounter at a bus stop results in the astonishing revelation of a former crack addict rescued by an anonymous benefactor. The housekeeper's odyssey commences when she runs away from a remote, poverty-stricken village wearing only one shoe and concludes not only with her daughter playing the violin in a music recital, but a documentation of the alarming number of child brides in Guatemala and a brief excursion into girls' names in Spanish.

A road trip across the state results in the shocking revelation that, in the 1920's, Seminole children were prohibited from attending either "white" or "colored" schools, but ends with an unexpected surprise: the Seminole Tribe of Florida, grown wealthy by the profits of its casinos, now owns the worldwide Hard Rock Café chain.

Some of the essays involved extensive research, often sparked by an apparently trivial observation; thus the story of the phony count and the fake countess begins when I noticed a sign with an inappropriate ampersand and leaps around the world to France, the former Belgian Congo, Yemen, the Emirate of Sharjah and Tangier.

It was not my purpose to write about the well-known, the rich or the famous, although a few of the characters herein were famous in their day, and some were even rich. Many of them deserve wider recognition: the Highwaymen's paintings once sold for $25 or $30, and Betty Mae Tiger Jumper's saga reads more like fiction than fact. The first two Jewish senators were pioneers in more ways than one, yet they have fallen into almost total obscurity.

They are Floridians, all, and some were even born in the Sunshine State. Yet most are transplants like me, native-born Americans migrating from elsewhere in the United States or immigrants fleeing Hitler's Germany, Castro's Cuba and the poverty of Guatemala. Each of them—each of us—possesses Real Stories to tell, and in this book the reader will discover some of them.

Despite my diligent fact-checking, errors may have crept into the text. Corrections or clarifications of any ambiguities are welcome. Readers can contact me at rwkenyon@gmail.com.

West Palm Beach
September 2016

"Mister Everything" Was an Imposter

I.

One of my best friends and his wife worked for twenty years at Aramco, the joint-venture between the government of Saudi Arabia and several American oil companies, the predecessors of ExxonMobil and Chevron. Created after the discovery of oil in Dhahran in 1938, its original purpose was to explore for, produce and export crude oil to the United States. My friend worked in the Training Department; he and his colleagues, Americans for the most part, taught English to Arabic-speaking employees of the company.[1]

One of my friend's colleagues was a lanky American from Savannah, Georgia, who went by the name of Robert "Bob" Hutchinson. Whenever you throw a bunch of expatriates who lived in Saudi Arabia into the same room, you are going to get a lot of story-telling and braggadocio. Bob's stories were among the most outlandish, but he recounted them with so much conviction, so much detail and

---

[1] The American managers at Aramco assiduously recruited young Saudis into the company. Ali al-Naimi, born in 1935, was hired as a tea-boy in 1947. Recognizing his abilities, the company financed his studies at the American University of Beirut, Lehigh and Stanford. Naimi served as Saudi minister of Petroleum and Mineral Resources from 1995 to 2016 and was named as one of the most influential people in the world by *Time* in 2008.

so much aplomb, that most people found Bob's stories believable and Bob himself irresistible.

On one occasion, Bob told his colleagues that he wouldn't be at work the next day because his father, a "famous American gynecologist," was flying into Dhahran in a private jet to deliver a baby for the wife of a Saudi prince. Granted the great wealth and the well-publicized excesses of the Saudi royalty, this story did not appear unnecessarily exaggerated.

Sometimes, however, Bob was caught making things up. One morning he came to work crying. He told the principal that he had to take the day off because his wife, Beverly, had just been diagnosed with cancer "from head to toe." That evening, however, as my friend and his wife were having dinner at the Aramco employees' dining hall, he spotted Bob and Beverly getting out of their car: the "cancer-ridden" Beverly was able to scamper nimbly up the steps unaided, the very picture of health. Another of Bob's outlandish stories is that he claimed to have performed "prostrate surgery" on a patient, not minding when people pointed out that the correct term was "prostate."

Bob told his colleagues that he was born in Savannah, Georgia, and went into great detail about local politicians and celebrities and other details that my friend could corroborate because he, too, had been born in that part of the Peach State. Despite that, Bob told his colleagues that English was not his native language. He explained that his

6

father, the same "famous gynecologist," had been a high-ranking officer during World War II, the right-hand man to General Douglas MacArthur during the post-war occupation of Japan, and the principal architect of the Japanese constitution. He added that he had learned Japanese while attending the same school as Crown Prince Akihito, the son of the reigning Emperor Hirohito. One of Bob's co-workers, however, told Bob that he had also studied Japanese, but had forgotten a lot of the vocabulary and asked him what the Japanese word for "house" was. "Uh, *puar-tu.*" The common Japanese term for "house" is *uchi.* Insofar as the Japanese constitution is concerned, it was drafted principally by two senior army officers with law degrees: Milo Rowell and Courtney Whitney, and implemented in 1946. Since Bob was born in 1939 it is extremely unlikely that he could have learned Japanese "as his first language" in a Japanese school, with or without the Emperor's son.

The Saudi trainees adored Bob. One of the reasons is that his classroom manner consisted exclusively of positive reinforcement: knowing that everyone loves praise, Bob never said an answer was wrong; it was right, but "can you think of something else to add?" He also applied Dale Carnegie's tip that a person's name is the sweetest sound that a person can hear: he memorized every trainee's name and always addressed them by name, pronounced properly.[2]

The English language examination consisted entirely of vocabulary questions. Because Bob had obtained the list of all the vocabulary terms, he didn't waste time on reading comprehension or written composition or other trivialities such as critical thinking: he "taught to the test," ensuring that most of the trainees passed with flying colors.

II.

On August 14, 1989, Joe Capozzi, a staff writer for the *Palm Beach Post*, reported that three days previously, an English teacher known as "Dr. H." and "Doc" among the students of the Lincoln Park Academy, in Fort Pierce, Florida, had been arrested on charges of fraud for allegedly using the names of a dead man and other people as his own. The arrested man claimed his name was Robert Hutchinson, but sheriff's deputies stated that his real name was Ralph Pierce Stregles and that the real Robert Hutchinson had died in 1975.

The Hutchinson-Stregles saga continued through the end of 1989 and all of 1990. Stregles pleaded guilty to passport fraud in federal court on January 31, 1990. He admitted using Hutchinson's name in an application to renew his passport in 1989. During the trial, he stated that he had been treated

---

[2] It is difficult for English-speakers to distinguish between Alaa, a first name meaning "greatness," and Allah, the word for God.

for "a mental illness" more than 25 years previously (which would have been some time before 1965) and that his wife had asked for a divorce. On April 23, 1990, Judge Marc Cianca told Stregles that his criminal case "reads like a good novel," then sentenced Stregles to five years' probation along with 500 hours of community service teaching adults how to read and write.

The last of the thirteen articles published in the *Palm Beach Post* appeared on February 15, 1991. That article stated that that the State of Florida had permanently revoked the teaching certificate of Stregles "a former St. Lucie County teacher who assumed another man's identity for 21 years."

III.

Ralph Pierce Stregles was born on June 5, 1939, in Savannah, Georgia, the seventh and youngest child of Albert E. and Clara Stregles. In the census of 1940, the ages of Ralph's four brothers and two sisters ranged from 19 to 3 years. After graduating from high school and majoring in English at Young Harris College in Young Harris, Georgia, Stregles transferred to Berry College in Mount Berry, Georgia, in 1960, where he befriended two of his classmates, Tom Chandler and John Burrell. According to Capozzi, writing in a lengthy article about Stregles published in the *Palm Beach Post* of September 3, 1989, Stregles, who had been placed on probation three times for failing grades, abruptly dropped out of Berry College in December 1962 "without even cleaning out his room." Stregles also testified in his trial that he had used the name "Tommy Chandler," but did not mention Burrell.

After serving briefly in the U.S. Navy, Stregles found employment in 1966 at Northwest Missouri State University in Maryville as an English teacher using the name of Tom Chandler, one of his classmates at Berry College. One of Stregles's colleagues in the English Department at Northwest Missouri was named Robert Hutchinson. The real Chandler, by then a student at Emory University in Atlanta, began receiving statements from a credit card that was not his and receipts for transcripts he had never ordered. Meanwhile, the administration at Northwest Missouri became suspicious when "Chandler" started bragging about being granted a Fulbright scholarship at a time of the year when the scholarships were not being awarded, and undertook an intensive investigation. In December 1967, the university president, Robert Foster, convoked Stregles and confronted him with the facts of his true identity. Capozzi quotes Foster stating that, "He just quietly left campus, and we left it at that."

The next year, Stregles showed up in Belton, South Carolina, where he taught at Belton–Honea Path High School using the name of John Burrell, another of his classmates at Berry College. When officials discovered he was an imposter, he resigned.

In 1969, using the passport he had obtained under the name of Robert Hutchinson, Stregles traveled to

Venezuela where he taught English at a school for Standard Oil employees in Caracas. For the next ten years, between 1971 and 1981 Stregles enrolled in graduate courses in Cleveland, Ohio, taught in Berea, Ohio and in Saint Thomas, Virgin Islands, obtained a doctorate at California Western University in San Diego and, still using Hutchinson's name, obtained a Florida teacher's certificate and taught at a high school in Fort Lauderdale before moving to Benghazi, Libya, where he became a member of the faculty at a university. Decidedly, Stregles had an advanced case of wanderlust.

In 1981, Stregles and Beverly, a former nun, relocated to Dhahran, Saudi Arabia, after he had obtained the teaching position at Aramco, where he met my friend. The couple returned to the United States in 1984 so that Beverly could receive medical treatment. After this point, we learn no more about her.

While in Houston, Ralph Stregles met a 62-year old retiree named Fred Kunce at the Briar Patch, advertised as "The Oldest Gay Bar in Houston." Shortly thereafter, Kunce invited Stregles to move into his ranch house in Cleveland, Texas, north of Houston, and introduced Stregles to his friends as "Doctor Hutchinson." Stregles recounted the same "prostrate surgery" story he had told my friend in Saudi Arabia. Kunce, born October 7, 1922, in Indiana, subsequently amended his will, designating Stregles as the sole beneficiary of his $175,000 estate and disinheriting the previous beneficiary,

11

June Dossat. Two months later, on May 1, 1985, Fred Kunce was discovered dead.

June Dossat then sued in July 1985 to overturn Kunce's will. Stregles left the country for a teaching job in Malaysia, and then returned to teach in New Orleans and Santa Fe, New Mexico. June Dossat's lawsuit went to trial in late 1986. The Harris County medical examiner's office ruled that Kunce died from accidental drowning after falling and hitting his head in his bathtub, but a Baylor University professor of pathology testified that Kunce's injuries were consistent with those that could result from a fall from a two-story building. Stregles's attorney countered that the professor had only read an autopsy report and had not examined Kunce's body, which had been cremated, perhaps upon the request of Stregles, Kunce's only heir and probable executor of the will. At the trial, Dossat testified, "I never met anyone who was Douglas Fairbanks and John D. Rockefeller all in one. He was Mister Everything." The probate judge dismissed questions about Kunce's death because no criminal charges had been filed. After the jurors reached a deadlock, the attorneys worked out a settlement dividing the estate between Dossat and Stregles.

IV.

In 1987 Stregles and his wife—perhaps it was Beverly, published accounts do not provide her first name—relocated to Saint Lucie County, Florida, where he would be hired as Dr. Robert Hutchinson at Lincoln Park Academy in Fort Pierce and where he was arrested on August 11, 1989. The evaluation in his personnel file was replete with effusive praise: "The effectiveness of Dr. Hutchinson's teaching is such that students perform better than they ever dreamed they could. I have seen no finer teacher." Stregles's Florida attorney, Osborne Walker O'Quinn, declared to the media, "My client in not a con man. He's one of those guys who, if they didn't pay him, he'd teach anyway." Outside the courtroom after his sentencing, Stregles told reporters that he felt betrayed: "I gave hundreds of hours of free work to [Lincoln Park] because I wanted their programs to look good, and the minute I was arrested [the teachers] all dumped me." He continued, "I have no regrets about anything I've done. I think society is too hung up on labels. Look at the number of people who have [diplomas] and can't function. The end product is what people should judge you on."

In its issue of Tuesday May 11, 1993, in an obituary datelined Brunswick, Georgia, the *Savannah Morning News* reported that Ralph Pierce Stregles, who was "employed by the Ramada Inn on Jekyll Island," died on May 7, 1993, at the age of fifty-three. "Surviving are four brothers, two sisters and several nieces and nephews."

A Mitzvah

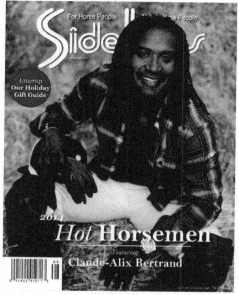

After spending ten years in Paris, I decided that the time had come for me to return to America.

In December 2014, I make a short trip to West Palm Beach and started looking for a place to live. After finding the apartment of my dreams, I still had a few days left to kill before returning to Paris to pack and ship my personal effects, so I drove out to The Mall at Wellington Green for some shopping and to run a few errands, one of which was to get an eye examination and purchase a new pair of eyeglasses. The optometrist put tropicamide drops in my eyes, so I decided to flip through the stack of magazines in the waiting room while my pupils dilated. One of them was the current issue of *Sidelines: For Horse People, About Horse People.*

The cover featured Haitian polo star Claude-Alix Bertrand, captain of Team Haiti and the subject of a profile by Doris Degner-Foster entitled "Hot, Haitian and on Fire." In perusing *Sidelines* for half an hour I gleaned enough information about horses and polo—especially about polo injuries—to satisfy a lifetime's curiosity:

> "I've broken my nose, my fingers, my pelvis and my wrists, but the biggest injury is when I broke my right leg. That leg now has seven pins and a couple of screws in it. It happened in the middle of the first season. I was waiting for a play and the horse got spooked by something, we don't know what. I got bucked over a fence and landed in the bleachers."

After my exam, I decided to have lunch before driving back to the hotel in order to allow the effects of the tropicamide to wear off, so I went into one of the restaurants in the mall, one of a "casual dining restaurant chain" serving American cuisine. I ordered what was described on the menu as a "Petite [sic] Sirloin."

Towards the end of the meal, Diana, the waitress, came back to my booth and asked in a confidential tone if I had noticed the couple seated diagonally across from me. *What an odd question,* I thought—and then it occurred to me that I might have missed Brad Pitt and Angelina Jolie enjoying a quiet lunch incognito among *hoi polloi.* Such a celebrity couple as "Brangelina" wouldn't have been out of place in

Wellington, since it's one of the few places on the planet where you can get a pick-up game of polo and where horses outnumber humans. "No," I answered, "I don't remember them. Were they young, old...?" "It was a middle-aged couple. They just paid for your lunch and wished you a Happy Holiday."

It's easy to imagine my astonishment, but I recovered quickly enough to wisecrack, "Well, Diana, you can cancel that "petite sirloin" and bring me the biggest steak in the house!" Then I explained to Diana what I thought had really happened. Although I'm not Jewish, there have been a lot of Jewish people in my life. I had learned from them the concept of the *mitzvah*, a moral deed performed as a religious duty. For Jews, God is pleased at such acts of human kindness, preferably performed anonymously. I reminded Diana that this was the holiday season not only for Christians, but for Jews—Hanukah—and that it was a season of gift-giving and celebration for believers of both faiths. I assured Diana that the couple must have been Jewish and that I had been the beneficiary of their generosity. Diana supported my hypothesis when she replied that she knew of several incidents recently where guests had paid for others' meals anonymously.

There was no way I could have thanked my benefactors or even have recognized them, since they had already left the restaurant. The only way for me to express my appreciation was to leave a generous tip for Diana. That would be my mitzvah.

BOGO

I.

Publix Super Markets, Inc., commonly known as Publix, is the largest chain of supermarkets in Florida. Founded in 1930 by George W. Jenkins, it is a private corporation headquartered in Lakeland, Florida. Ownership of Publix stock is restricted to current or former employees or board members, and shares can not be sold outside the company without first being offered to the company for repurchase. Eighty percent of the shares are owned by the company's employees; the founding family only retains 20% of the equity in the firm. All employees who have put in 1,000 work hours and a year of employment receive an additional 8.5% of their total pay in the form of stock. Dividends are paid quarterly.

In 2016, Publix was operating 1,111 stores throughout six states in the Southeast, including 764 locations in Florida and in 2014 the company was ranked number 75 on *Fortune* magazine's list of the 100 Best Companies to Work for in America and number 8 on the *Forbes* magazine 2014 list of America's Largest Private Companies. It is also the largest privately-owned company in Florida.

The chain, with over 166,000 employees, has a reputation for the high level of its customer service. On one occasion, I went to the Customer Service desk to ask where the batteries and envelopes were located; instead of telling me which aisles they were on, the Publix associate escorted me personally to each location and then rang up my purchases herself.

Publix however, is neither a food coöp nor a charitable organization like the Salvation Army; its management and employees run the business to make a profit and the company is the country's most profitable grocer. Furthermore, the family of Mr. Jenkins has become quite wealthy, and *Forbes* reports that two of Mr. Jenkins's children, Carol Jenkins Barnett and Howard M. Jenkins, are billionaires.

I recently went shopping at a Publix near where I live. When I put my purchases on the check-out conveyor belt, the customer ahead of me, an attractive, middle-aged woman ahead of me wearing a chic black skirt and matching top, noticed that I was buying a package of ground buffalo meat. "It's quite tasty," I told her, "It has less fat and more flavor. The animals graze free-range and munch grasses. They have organic beef, and I've bought organic eggs, butter, bread and peanut butter, too. But they don't have nearly as many organic foods as in the Carrefour in Paris where I used to shop." "I understand," the lady replied, "I used to live in Switzerland." We exchanged knowing looks.

"But Americans," I replied, "Especially young people, are demanding healthier food, and chains offering organic food are booming whereas some of the fast-food chains are hemorrhaging customers."

Then I noticed the items she had placed on the conveyor belt. "I see you've got a real French camembert cheese there; I know what *you* like."

"It's the only thing my daughter will eat," was her surprising reply. I thought, *what rich taste!* She continued, "Have you been to the specialty cheese department at Publix on Palm Beach Island? Nestor is in charge of the cheeses and is very knowledgeable." She must have been a frequent customer since the two were on a first-name basis. I later looked up an article on the reopening of the Palm Beach Publix and, although Nestor wasn't mentioned, I learned that the wine steward, Rudy, had been in charge of his department for "close to three decades."

"And this," the lady continued, pointing to a quart of Welch's Dragon Fruit Mango Fruit Juice Cocktail Blend, "Is for my son; he's sick, and this is the only thing he will drink." *What is Dragon Fruit?* I thought. I should have thought, *What odd children.*

I looked up Dragon Fruit as soon as I could. It seems that it is more precisely defined as the pitaya, [*Hylocereus undatus*]. The tree is indigenous to Central America but is also grown in and exported from several Southeast Asian countries, such as Thailand and Vietnam.

Obtained from a species of cactus, sweet pitayas have a creamy pulp and a delicate aroma. The pitaya blooms only at night; the large white fragrant flowers are called "moonflower" or "Queen of the Night."

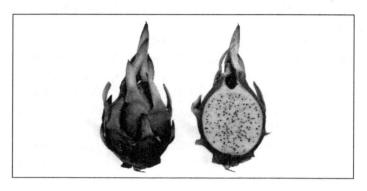

II.

Lindeman's is an Australian winery, founded in 1843 by Dr. Henry John Lindeman (1811-1881), an English surgeon, who had visited the wine districts of France and Germany in the 1830's and studied their wines and production methods. Dr. Lindeman and his wife, née Eliza Bramhall, migrated to Australia in 1840 and planted the first vines in the Hunter Valley of New South Wales: the corporate logo on the label proclaims *Felicitas in vitæ 1843*. Lindeman's now owns vineyards in South Australia and is considered a mass-producer of reasonably priced, good quality wine, exporting to twenty-two countries. In 1993, its "iconic" Bin 65 chardonnay was Australia's top-selling white wine export. Five consecutive vintages were named "best buys" by *The Wine Spectator*, and the American wine guru

Robert M. Parker, Jr., declared it "one of the three or four finest chardonnay values in the world" in his newsletter. Lindeman's[3] was acquired in 2005 by Treasury Wine Estates, the wine division of Australian beverage conglomerate Foster's Group, acquired, in turn, by SABMiller in 2011.

The Publix had a promotion on Lindeman's wines: "Buy One Get One Free," for which they have coined an acronym, "BOGO." The price for the Lindeman's wines was two bottles for the price of $5.99 + 6% Florida sales tax. To me, however, the slogan should have been, "Two for the Price of One" or even "Half Price." But there's a subtle difference between these phrases, and understanding that nuance is key to understanding American mass psychology.

Many French people consider us Americans overgrown children; in fact, in 1979, a novelist named Claude Courchay published a book with the title *Les Américains sont de grands enfants.* Perhaps he has a point. Just as American children believe in Santa Claus and the Tooth Fairy, many American adults like to believe that you can get things for free, that it's possible to get something for nothing. Americans even believe that they can wage wars for free. On February 9, 2004, President

---

[3] Lindeman's with the apostrophe should not be confused with Lindemans without it. The latter is a family-owned brewery located in Vlezenbeek, Belgium, where the Lindemans family has specialized in producing award-winning, spontaneously-fermented lambic ales since 1822.

George W. Bush described himself on *Meet the Press* as a "war president," even though Congress had never declared war against Iraq as the Constitution requires: Article I, Section 8, Clause 11 of the United States Constitution vests in the Congress the sole power to declare war, not the president. At any rate, Bush's government bombarded, invaded, occupied and destroyed the sovereign nation of Iraq, a country that never posed any threat whatsoever to the United States. At the same time, during his tenure, George W. Bush signed four laws cutting Americans' taxes, and those laws were extended under President Barack Obama. Despite those tax cuts, Americans still complained that their taxes were too high.

The Three Trillion Dollar War is the title of a book published in 2008 by Professor Joseph Stieglitz, a Nobel Prize winning economist and former chief economist of the World Bank, and Linda Blimes. That amount is their estimate of the full cost of the Iraq War, including many hidden expenditures, such as lifetime medical care for over 670,000 disabled veterans. Yet most Americans believed that they fought the Iraq War for free, just as the Publix customers believed they got those bottles of Lindeman's wine for free.

Economic historian Hugh Rockoff of Rutgers explains in *The U.S. Economy in World War I*, an essay published by the Economic History Association, that wars can be financed in only three ways: (1) raising taxes (2) borrowing from the public and (3) printing money. The Iraq war was

24

financed, not by imposing a war tax or borrowing from the American public in the form of war bonds, but by borrowing from China and by issuing billions of dollars of fiat money.

In that light, we can understand why, according to the Publix promotion, customers believed they were getting a bottle free when, in reality, they were just paying half price for each bottle—buying each for $2.99. The customers simply deluded themselves into believing that one bottle was free. I took advantage of the promotion and, over a few days, bought bottles of Bin 65 chardonnay, Bin 40 merlot, Bin 45 cabernet sauvignon and Bin 50 shiraz—that's the same grape the French know as syrah and use in making Côtes du Rhône. All those wines are easy to drink; I found none exceptional. At a price of $2.99 per bottle, however, they were excellent value for money.

A week or two after the "BOGO" promotion, I saw that Publix had launched a new promotion: four bottles of Lindeman's wine for $12.00. "They sent me pallets of the stuff," the Grocery Manager told me. But all they had was chardonnay and pinot grigio. The store was out of reds: no merlot, no shiraz, no cabernet sauvignon. "Maybe tomorrow," he told me encouragingly.

I can't think of the last time I drank pinot grigio—the French call it pinot gris—so I put four bottles of that "iconic" Bin 65 chardonnay in my shopping cart. But I also picked up two coupons, each good for an immediate refund of one dollar off a bottle of

Lindeman's wine. At the end, I walked out of the store with four bottles of very drinkable wine shipped from over 15,000 kilometers (almost 10,000 miles) away for a total of $10.00+tax.

The next day, I returned to the store hoping to find some Lindeman's reds. The cabernet sauvignon and the shiraz were available at the promotional price, but there wasn't any merlot. Merlot is my favorite red wine because Pétrus, the legendary wine from the Pomerol area of the Bordelais, is made from merlot grapes. Whenever I quaff merlot I imagine it's Pétrus in my glass.[4] When I expressed my disappointment to Edna, the cashier at the checkout aisle, she helpfully suggested that I ask Customer Service for a rain check.

If you're not an American, you will probably not know what a rain check is, because its origins, dating back to the 1870's, lie in the quintessential American sport, baseball. Tickets to baseball games, which are played in outdoor stadiums, have three parts: one section is detached at the gate, the

---

[4] Although commonly referred to as "Château" Pétrus, there is no château on the estate, just an ordinary two-story farmhouse built in the eighteenth century.

other two—the receipt and the rain check—are retained by the spectator.

If the game is cancelled because of rain—or for any other unforeseeable circumstance—the rain check grants the bearer free admission to the rescheduled game.

By analogy, a rain check issued by merchandisers is a voucher allowing a customer to purchase an out-of-stock item at a later date for the same promotional price. I had thirty days to use my rain check to buy four bottles of wine for $12.00.

I thought that this was the end of the story, but on my next visit, I was in for yet another surprise: hanging around the neck of each bottle was a coupon for an immediate refund of $2.00, thereby reducing the price to only $1.00 a bottle. The store management had conveniently posted a sign showing the arithmetic for the convenience of the mathematically challenged.

At the rate they are unloading this inventory, I expect that, before long, the Grocery Manager will be accosting his customers and paying them to take the "stuff" off his hands: "Here's a couple of bucks, buddy; just grab a bottle or two and scram!"

My New Telephone

One morning, the Cable Guy, Wayne, came and hooked up the Wi-Fi modem and the land line. In scrounging around the apartment I had rented, I discovered a ten-year old VTech T2240 cordless telephone, the type with the external antenna mounted on top. I connected it to the modem and

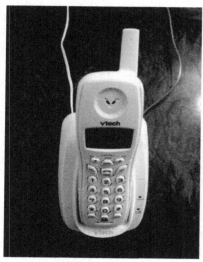 plugged in the transformer, then I asked Wayne to test the line by calling me from his cell phone. The phone rang, all right, but the clarity and tone were mediocre; I could barely understand him. Then I started realizing that I had been frequently asking people to repeat what they said and that when I use my smartphone, I always turn on the speaker. It dawned on me that, like most people, as I had aged, my hearing had deteriorated. I needed a new telephone.

That afternoon, I went to the Mandel Public Library of West Palm Beach. As I exited the elevator, I almost crashed into an attractive brunette holding a poster; her name I learned to be Valerie.

"Would you like a free telephone?"

What kind of encounter is this? I thought. *Was she a* hada madrina, *a fairy godmother, who had read my thoughts and suddenly thrust herself into my life, waylaying me in order to grant me my wish?*

"Sure," I answered, "Are you handing them out? I actually do need a new telephone." Her sign indicated that people with impaired hearing could qualify to receive an amplified telephone, courtesy of the State of Florida.

"You need to go upstairs to the third floor—just follow the signs—and be screened. If you qualify, you get your telephone."

This was too good to be true. To the Spanish playwright Pedro Calderón de la Barca, *la vida es sueño*—life is a dream. Was I living a dream? Back upstairs I went, following the signs to a small conference room. I was greeted by Valerie's colleague, Keith, who asked me if I had a hard time hearing on the telephone. I recounted what had happened when the Cable Guy had called me on the VTech and the other signs I had noticed of hearing impairment. This qualified me to receive a free telephone.

Keith described four telephones on the table, each equipped with volume and tone controls to amplify the sound and increase the clarity. Two were standard models with the keypad and controls on the body and a handset connected to the body with a coiled cord. Both had oversized keys; one of them with eight additional keys for speed-dialing frequently-called numbers and little windows where users could insert names or pictures. The other two were cordless; one had a screen to display caller ID. Three of the four were equipped with a transformer to convert 110-Volt AC current to the 8-Volt DC current required to power the telephones. One derived its power from the phone line itself. Keith explained that this feature could be useful during the spring and summer when bolts of lightning often knock out the electricity in southeastern Florida.

I was then asked to test the four telephones by listening to a pre-recorded message of a male and a female voice and then, after adjusting the voice and tone, select the one in which the voices were the clearest. I picked the phone with the picture keys, a ClearSounds 500.

I then was asked to show proof that I was a permanent resident of the State of Florida. Out of my wallet came my State of Florida driver's license.

II.

Unlike almost every other country, the United States government does not issue national identity cards. Since the United States, like Switzerland and Canada, is a federation, each state government enjoys a large measure of autonomy, including the power to issue driver's licenses. These documents

31

are customarily, but bizarrely used for identification purposes.

According to the Wikipedia, "All legislative attempts to create a national identity card have failed due to tenacious opposition from both liberal and conservative politicians, who regard the national identity card as the mark of a totalitarian society."

Starting on July 14, 2008, however, it has been possible for American citizens to obtain a credit-card sized biometric Passport Card, used for land and sea travel between the United States and Canada, Mexico, the Caribbean and Bermuda. The cards can be ordered at the same time as a passport is renewed for a cost of $30.00. The Passport Card is *de facto* a national identity card and almost ten million had been issued through 2015. Furthermore, the 50 states and the six territories issue their own identification cards to people who are either too young to drive, who are unable to drive or do not wish to drive. Applying the politicians' ridiculous logic, we may therefore conclude that all these governments are totalitarian.

After filling in a form, Keith packed the phone and handed the box over to me, explaining that it was mine to use on a long-term basis at no cost as long as I remained in Florida. If I left the state, I had to return it. He included the instruction booklet in English, Spanish and French. "Not Haitian Creole?" I queried, "It's the third most commonly spoken

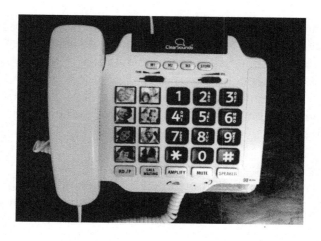

language in southern Florida." "Not yet and, besides, a lot of Haitians speak French."

As I was preparing to leave, Valerie arrived in time to congratulate me on receiving my new telephone.

III.

But that was not the end of the story. After Wayne, the Cable Guy, had installed and activated my phone line that morning and was packing up his equipment and preparing to leave, the phone rang. I assumed it was the telecom company—which shall remain nameless, although I found out later that it's high on the list of the most hated companies in America—calling to test the line, so I told Wayne to answer it. Nobody knew my phone number, so the call could not possibly have been for me. Wayne picked up the receiver and, after short silence, hung up. "Who was it?" I inquired. With a befuddled look, Wayne replied that it was a robocall, an automated call from a computerized device that automatically dials telephone numbers and delivers a recorded message from a telemarketer. Many, but not all, robocalls are illegal. I couldn't believe it: the line had been operational for less than five minutes and I was already being pestered by a robocall!

It proved to be the first of many. Before long, I started receiving unwanted calls from real live human telemarketers as well. I promptly acquired the habit of simply not answering the phone when it rang, assuming that if the call was from someone I knew, that person would just call me back on my cell phone. Then I realized that, by not answering the phone, I had defeated the purpose of even having one.

Furthermore, although I made almost no phone calls myself, the charges on the incomprehensible three-page monthly statements from the phone company varied from $74.38 to $129.05. After four months, I had had enough. I called the phone company and cancelled the service. I realized that, in twenty-first-century America, a smartphone was quite sufficient, and that there was no need to have a land line just to be bombarded with robocalls and solicitations by aggressive telemarketers. Disconsolate, I returned my new telephone.

There was, however, a happy end to this story. To my great surprise, a few weeks after I had cancelled the service, I received a check in the mail from the phone company for $35.75. It seems they had finally figured out that I had overpaid my bill. Along with the check was a form letter informing me that if I wished a "clarification" of the refund, I could call a toll-free number. I can assure you that this is a number I will never call for the rest of my life: they might have figured out in the meantime that they had sent me the check in error and demand that I send the money back.

Enemies, a Love Story

I.

Isaac Bashevis Singer was born in the Polish shtetl of Leoncin, near Warsaw, on November 21, 1902. Aware of the rise of Nazism in Germany, Singer emigrated from Poland to join his brother Joshua in New York City in 1935, abandoning his common-law wife Runia Pontsch and five-year old son Israel. Runia and Israel emigrated first to Moscow, then to Palestine, where Israel Hebraicized his surname to Zamir, Hebrew for "singer," and spent the next eighty years of his life on a kibbutz. He did not meet his father again until 1955, during a brief visit to New York. [5]

In New York, Singer took up work as a journalist and columnist for the *Jewish Daily Forward,* a Yiddish-language newspaper. In 1938, he met a Jewish refugee from Munich, Alma Wassermann. They married in 1940.

Singer published 18 novels, 14 children's books, and a number of memoirs, essays and articles. He is best known as a writer of short stories, which have been published in more than a dozen collections.

---

[5] Israel Zamir died on November 22, 2014, at the age of 85. Joshua Singer died on February 10, 1944. The date and location of Runia's death are unknown at this time.

Singer won the Nobel Prize in Literature in 1978, the first laureate in that category who wrote only in Yiddish, a dialect of medieval German originating in the ninth century, written in Hebrew characters and considered the historic language of the Ashkenazi Jews of Central Europe. Singer's advocacy and defense of Yiddish were instrumental in keeping this language alive. After spending most of his life in Manhattan, Singer became a Floridian, moving to Surfside, near Miami, where he died on July 24, 1991.

II.

Enemies, A Love Story, a novel written in 1972, takes place in 1949 in three locations in New York City: Coney Island, the Bronx and the Lower East Side. Herman Broder, the anti-hero of the story, is a Holocaust survivor who finds himself married to three wives. Yadwiga is an illiterate and "simple" Polish peasant who sheltered him in the hayloft of her barn to protect him from the Nazis. Despite the fact that Yadwiga is Catholic, Broder has married her as much out of gratitude as from love, and brought her to America.

Masha, another Holocaust survivor and a divorcée, lives with her mother in the Bronx and is a provocative and promiscuous mistress who manipulates her lover into marrying her in a Jewish ceremony, even though the marriage is invalid.

As Broder is shuttling between his two wives, pretending to be a traveling salesman on business trips to Philadelphia, Tamara arrives on the scene. She is Broder's first wife and the mother of his two children, but Broder believes she was executed by the Nazis back in Poland: "There were witnesses," Broder laments to Rabbi Lampert, whose sermons he ghost-writes. In fact, Tamara has survived, still bearing the bullet in her body, although the children perished. In the disconcerting conclusion, although one of the three wives has committed suicide and another has given birth, Broder is nowhere to be seen. He has simply evaporated; it's as if he never existed. Now it's the women's Real Story alone.

In 1989, the novel was adapted for the screen by writer-director Paul Mazursky and starred Ron Silver as Broder and Anjelica Huston as Tamara. The Palm Beach Opera performed a world premiere of a musical version of the novel on February 20-22, 2015, at the Kravis Center for the Performing Arts.

The cast, sets and costumes were all outstanding. Supertitles projected on a screen helped the audience understand the text, although they were superfluous since the libretto was written in English and the acoustics were excellent. Additionally, a video wall designed by Greg Emetaz projected mosaics of contemporary billboards, buildings and memorabilia as a visual counterpoint to the action on stage.

After the performance, I ran a search for reviews on the internet and found three; two were generally positive, but the third, by Lawrence Budman, published in the *South Florida Classical Review* dismissed the work: "Despite the earnest efforts of the cast and creative team…the piece emerged as a tedious clunker, leavened by fleeting moments of lyrical inspiration."

Budman disliked the score by Ben Moore: "Much of the score sounds contrived and ineffective. The string-heavy orchestral score is lushly orchestrated in the best Hollywood style. Moore's attempts at introducing Judaic elements sometimes fall flat... The klezmer band that played in the Kravis lobby before the performance and during intermission was more authentic and a lot more fun."

I, too, was disappointed by the music. Moore states in the program notes that he was influenced by the music of George Gershwin and Kurt Weill, citing *Porgy and Bess* and *Mahagonny*, but there is nothing lyrical in his three-hour score. There are no real songs; there are no melodies that you can hum as you leave the theater. With *Porgy and Bess* and *Mahagonny*, you can sing the whole thing: I have and I do—in the privacy of my home, of course.

Budman also disliked the libretto by Nahma Sandrow, describing it as "long-winded," but here I disagree. I liked the text and appreciated the many passages of introspection articulating the moral dilemma confronting the paranoid and desperate protagonist. After all, Broder is a Jew who finds himself with three wives on his hands, one of whom is a Gentile and, if that weren't enough, bigamy is a felony. That's ample cause for most men to become paranoid and desperate.

Although the story is set among survivors of the Holocaust and is suffused with Jewish elements in both the libretto and the score—citations from the Torah and excerpts from cantorial music—perhaps the opera's finest achievement is that one doesn't have to be Jewish to appreciate Singer's tale. There is a universality about the characters' predicament that anyone can understand and, in a sense, the plot could have been dramatized by a classical Greek playwright or a Shakespeare.

III.

Bigamy is not as rare as we might imagine. From time to time we read of men who have maintained multiple wives and families for many years and whose duplicity is only revealed by some minor or unpredictable event: the trace of perfume or lipstick on clothing or an impromptu encounter. Such a case was reported in February 2015 in Oklahoma: a suspected bigamist was identified and arrested because of a selfie that his first wife posted on Facebook. Shortly thereafter, the second wife noticed the picture and contacted the first wife via the website. "She asked me why I had her husband on my page and I said, 'No this is my husband,'" declared wife number one. It was subsequently determined that the alleged philanderer had married his first wife in 2002 and the second in 2012. "I'm glad the guy is going to jail because he made my life miserable," the first wife told a reporter for KFOR News.

There are women bigamists, too. In 2009, the media in the United Kingdom reported the case of 30-year old Mancunian Emily Horne, a "predatory female" who had married on five occasions but never divorced. As in most things, even in bigamy, the ladies outdo us men.

Later on, I watched the trailer to Paul Mazursky's film on the internet. The film adaptation appeared to convey a range of emotions—hot sex and hotter anger doused with cold showers of comic relief— lacking in the operatic version. I want to see it. I want to read Singer's novel too, but I'll settle for the English translation.

"I ran away from home with only one shoe"

This is the Real Story of Milagros, a housekeeper.

I.

I was born and raised in a family of ten children in a small village near the town of Quetzaltenango in rural, western Guatemala. There are twenty-four recognized, national, indigenous languages in Guatemala. My father spoke K'iche' and my mother Mam. K'iche' is spoken by around a million people and Mam by around half a million. Because my parents spoke different native languages, they communicated in Spanish, the official language of the country, and my siblings and I spoke Spanish with each other and with our parents. I also learned to speak Mam with my mother and still speak it. All twelve of us lived under one roof in a two-room shanty. Since we always ran barefoot around the house, we had no need for shoes except when going to market. My father bought a pair of plastic shoes for 6 quetzales, the equivalent then of one dollar, that we shared and used as needed.

At the age of twelve I learned from a girl from my village that there was work in Guatemala City, the capital. Since my father was opposed to the idea of my leaving home, I decided to run away after completing the sixth grade. I put in a little bag my most precious possession, a *traje*, the national costume for women in Guatemala, a two-piece outfit composed of an overblouse known as a *huipil* and a wraparound skirt called a *corte*. Every village has its own style of *traje*. The designs go back to the Mayas, my ancestors.

I knew I would need the shoes in Guatemala City but, as I was running late for the bus, I lost one of them on the way. Normally, unaccompanied children could not travel on the buses, so when the conductor asked where my mother was, I said she was sitting in the back. I bought a one-way ticket and left home wearing only one shoe. In the capital I found work as a housecleaner, working seven days a week for the equivalent of five dollars a month. As soon as I had saved up enough money, I bought a pair of shoes—leather shoes, not plastic shoes—for 70 quetzales. That was the happiest day of my life. Eventually, I found live-in employment with a couple; the husband was Irish and his wife Guatemalan. They decided to move to Miami to go into business and I followed them on my own. Unfortunately, during the stock market crash of 2008, their business went bankrupt. They got divorced. He returned to Ireland and she to Guatemala. I was on my own. But by that time I was fifteen, already married to a fellow Guatemalan and the mother of a daughter. Eventually I, too, divorced.

Although my parents were disappointed that I had dropped out of school and angry at my leaving home, we have reconciled. I call them once a month. Since they don't have a telephone, my father walks half an hour in a new pair of plastic shoes to the house of a distant neighbor who has a telephone and schedules a call: your daughter must call you at such-and-such a time on such-and-such a day. I pay for the calls by the minute.

I am studying hard in order to pass my GED exam in order to attend college. The test lasts seven hours! In the meantime, for the last seven years I have continued cleaning houses, and my daughter is taking violin lessons: her teacher tells me she's quite gifted. Imagine that back in Quetzaltenango!

II.

Stephanie Sinclair, founder and executive director of the nonprofit organization Too Young to Wed, stated in an article entitled "Child, Bride, Mother," in the February 6, 2015, issue of the *New York Times Sunday Review* that "Child marriage is pervasive in more than 50 countries, with girls in rural areas of developing nations especially vulnerable." Sinclair cites data compiled by the Population Council that in the villages of Guatemala, around 53 percent of women age 20 to 24 were married before age 18, and 13 percent before 15, adding that, "In Guatemala, it's legal for a girl to marry as young as 14—though many are married far younger than that."

Thousands of young girls in rural villages of Central American countries like Guatemala are married off as child brides and condemned to an existence of squalor and ignorance, often withdrawing from their education as early as elementary school. These girls are often subject to physical and sexual violence and some even die due to complications of teenage pregnancy and lack of crucial prenatal care. Sinclair observed that among the girls she interviewed in the Petén region of northern Guatemala, "Other times, the girls' problems began only after making it home with their babies, where they were frequently abandoned by their husbands."

Sinclair's article concludes, "The United Nations Population Fund estimates that in 2015 more than 550,000 Guatemalan girls [would] marry before they are 18. That's 1,500 girls married every day in just one country."

Milagros is an exception because she benefitted from an awareness of the cruel fate awaiting her if she had remained in her village; she had summoned the courage to seek her independence and forge a life for herself and her daughter.

III.

Perhaps Milagros owes part of her success to her name: *milagros* translates as "miracles" in English, and it would be no exaggeration to conclude that she has benefited from a number of miracles in her life. Hers is one of a number of Spanish girls' names whose meaning is more than casual. Some are named Remedios, meaning "remedies," Consuelo, meaning "comfort" and Amparo meaning "protection." Other names are inspired by nature: Lirio means "lily," Rocio means "dew" and Sol means "sun." Just as some French girls are named "France," some Latinas are named "América." There are even girls named Magos, meaning "magicians," "wizards" or "wise men." Magos Herrera is a Mexican jazz singer. Perhaps girls named Dolores, meaning "sorrows," were so named because their mothers underwent a difficult childbirth.

The Phony Count and the Fake Countess

I.

One Tuesday, I went to vote. The polling place for my precinct was in a building on the campus shared by the Dreyfoos School of the Arts and Palm Beach State College. After I left the polls proudly sporting my "I Voted. Did You?" sticker on my shirt, I noticed a two-story structure with an astonishing name: The Count & Countess de Hoernle Building. Having lived in France for many years, I have known a few counts and countesses in my day, but I had never heard of any de Hornles. Furthermore, "de Hoernle" didn't look very French. What surprised me the most is that a count and countess would emblazon their names—linked absurdly with an ampersand—on such an unprepossessing building. An ampersand? I smelled a rat.

II.

As soon as I got home, I ran a search for "de Hoernle." What I found was a story that easily confirms the dictum that the truth is far stranger than fiction.

According to the 1940 Census records, Adolph Hoernle was a German, born "about 1903," who lived on the Grand Concourse in the Bronx, New York. His wife, Louise, was also born in Germany, "about 1900." No mention of a title for either one.

As I continued my search, I learned from newspaper articles that an Adolph Hoernle (or Hörnle) was born on May 10, 1903, in Pforzheim. According to a "family biography" quoted in one article, Adolph "earned his degree as an engineer in 1923 and emigrated to the United States in 1926." He amassed a fortune from the Stewart Stamping Corp., a tool-and-die company that he founded in Yonkers, New York, and sold in 1965. Although married in 1940 to Louise (whose maiden name I never discovered), she appears to have disappeared from sight during World War II, since Adolph married a woman named Henrietta Rach on October 26, 1950. The couple settled in Bronxville, a posh Westchester County suburb of New York, and raised two daughters. It thus appears that Louise and Henrietta are two distinct individuals.

50

After selling his company and traveling the world, Adolph and Henrietta bought a house in 1981 in Boca Raton, Florida, thereafter splitting their time between "Boca," as it's known in the local parlance, and New York. The couple moved to Florida permanently in 1989 and began devoting their efforts and their fortune to underwriting and subsidizing scores of philanthropic activities and endeavors, notably financing the construction of buildings in and near Boca Raton, including the building I had seen on the Dreyfoos campus. In one article, the couple's attorney, Alan Kauffman, estimated that in eleven years his clients had given local charities and needy persons more than $10 million. Adolph Hoernle died on September 10, 1998, at the age of 95, survived by his wife, his two daughters and nine grandchildren.

III.

A dithyrambic tribute published in 2012 on the occasion of her 100th birthday stated that Henrietta, Countess de Hoernle, was born in Karlsruhe, Germany, on September 24, 1912. Another biography published on a website devoted to her[6] states that "Her mother, Theresa, was a violinist, and her father, George, was a pianist." The tribute states that she emigrated to America in 1931 aboard the S.S. Pennland to live with her grandparents in Jackson Heights, Brooklyn [sic].[7] The article also states that Henrietta was twice widowed before

---

[6] www.countess100.org

[7] Jackson Heights is located in the Borough of Queens.

marrying Adolph: her first husband, Karl Heinz Bisping, with whom she had a daughter, "died in an accident." A second husband, Jeff Gass, with whom she had another daughter, "served in the U.S. Army during World War II and contracted malaria in the South Pacific." The article further states that Gass "was in charge of all the documents for the Nuremberg trials" and that he died in 1949, "from complications of his malarial condition [sic]." A search of New York state records produces no result for either Karl Heinz Bisping or Jeff Gass, and a search of military legal resources in the Library of Congress data base reveals no data for a Jeff Gass. If we add the two daughters Henrietta had with Adolph and the two she had with Bisping and Gass, it would appear that Henrietta was the mother of four daughters, yet only two are cited in her biographical sketches. Perhaps there really were only two.

Henrietta stated that she met Adolph Hoernle at a masquerade ball in 1950 hosted by the Liederkranz Club, where she stated she had met her previous husbands. Founded in 1847, the club is a social organization now known as the Liederkranz of the City of New York and is devoted to cultural and social exchange and the sponsorship of musical events.

Adolph and Henrietta pursued their philanthropic activities in and around Boca Raton as ordinary citizens until 1981 when they suddenly began to refer to themselves as the Count and Countess de Hoernle. Henrietta, known to her friends as "Rita," was particularly fond of wearing tiaras and sashes at social events.

The Hoernles had now added an aristocratic French particle to Adolph's decidedly proletarian moniker to become the *de* Hoernles. Since they were both German, however, it would have been more logical for them to have called themselves *von* Hoernle. But there is not much logic in this story.

Nevertheless, everything seemed to be smooth sailing for the next decade until a fateful day in 1992 when Wayne L. Ezell, the editor of the *Boca Raton News* and reporter Sharon Geltner published a front-page lead story on February 26 claiming that the de Hoernles' titles were fakes, purchased in 1981 for $20,000 "from a huckster."

The outcry was immediate and violent: According to an article published in *Editor & Publisher* on April 25, 1992, Henrietta was so infuriated by the story that she threatened to "cut local charities out of $22 million in her will." She also demanded an apology from the newspaper and urged dismissal of Ezell and Geltner.

The newspaper was deluged with letters and phone calls, mostly highly critical of its treatment of the couple. Twenty-eight readers cancelled their subscriptions. Supporters bought full-page ads to proclaim "support, appreciation and respect to the Count and Countess de Hoernle."

IV.

But let's return to 1981 when Adolph and Henrietta were suddenly transmogrified into the Count and Countess de Hoernle. The "Countess" herself inadvertently provided the key in an interview she gave to station WJNO in West Palm Beach on February 28, 1992, two days after the front-page article appeared: "I was given the title by Prince Alexis d'Anjou. D'Anjou's full name is Prince Alexis d'Anjou de Bourbon Condé Romanov-Dolgorouky." One doesn't need to waste time consulting Burke's Peerage to know that the comic-opera title of this "prince" is as phony as a three-dollar bill. Ezell and Geltner were right: Henrietta and Adolph were the victims—willing or not—of a con artist.

Who was Prince Alexis d'Anjou de Bourbon Condé Romanov Dolgorouky?

This is where the story moves if not from reality into fiction at least into surrealism. A search on the Wikipedia reveals that the "prince" was born Alexis Ceslaw Maurice Jean Brimeyer on May 4, 1946, in Costermansville, in the former Belgian Congo, now present-day Bukuvu, in the Democratic Republic of the Congo, to Victor Alfred August Brimeyer, an agronomist from Luxembourg, and a Belgian, Beatrice Czapska (*alias* Beatrice de Fonzi). The lead paragraph of the Wikipedia article states that Brimeyer was "a false pretender who claimed connection to various European thrones. He used fraudulent combined titles like Prince d'Anjou Durazzo Durassow Romanoff Dolgorouki de Bourbon-Condé. He also sold false titles of nobility through 'orders' he and his associates had created." Brimeyer was nicknamed the Congolese Conman.

Insofar as the Hoernles are concerned, Henrietta collected memberships in a number of the phony orders of chivalry of the type that Brimeyer produced and promoted, all of which are just as fake as her title. As reported in *The Epoch Times* on July 5, 2009, "In addition to her title of Countess, she has seven Dame titles: Dame de Grande Croix de Justice: Ordre Militaire et Hospitalier de Notre Dame du Mont Carmel; Dame of the Noble Companion of the Swan; Dame of the Knightly Association of St. George the Martyr; Dame of the Sovereign Military Order of the Temple of Jerusalem; Dame of the Most Venerable and Holy Order of Saint Basil the Great; Dame Commander of Justice of the Order of the Knights of Malta, Holder of the Grand Cross; Dame Commander of

Justice, Ambassador at Large, Order of St. John of Jerusalem, Knights of Malta." A web search will reveal that all these are either modern imitations of defunct orders or slightly altered names of existing chivalric orders.

During Brimeyer's entire life he attempted to ennoble himself. When he was ten, he dubbed himself Brimeyer de la Calchuyère. Several of the titles he concocted or usurped resulted in lawsuits by legitimate nobility; in one of these trials, in Belgium, the Princesses Khevenhuller-Abensberg and Maria Dolgoroukoff and Prince Alexander Pavlovich Dolgorouki lodged a complaint against Brimeyer, accusing him of using the titles of Prince Khevenhuller-Abensberg and Prince Romanov-Dolgorouki as well as the name Brimeyer-Abensberg with malicious intent. The trial resulted in Brimeyer's conviction on November 24, 1971, and a sentence of 18 months in jail, which he avoided by absconding to Greece, where he produced phony documents attempting to prove that he was a direct descendent of the emperors of Byzantium.

In 1979 Brimeyer was in Spain and attempted to be recognized as a member of the house of Anjou-Durazzo. In 1982 he published a book in French, *Moi, Alexis, arrière-petit-fils du tsar,* under the name of Prince Alexis d'Anjou Romanov-Dolgorouki, Duke of Durazzo. This is the phony title that Henrietta cited in her radio interview in 1992, in which she unwittingly revealed the hoax.

56

V.

And this brings us to yet another royal imposter. In 1984, Brimeyer's mother joined her son in his fraudulent activities. She renamed herself Princess Olga Beatrice Nikolaevna Romanovskaia Dolgoroukaia, Princess of the Ukraine, Countess of Fonzo, and married an American named Bruce Chalmers, born on December 5, 1913. Chalmers referred to himself as both Alfonso Yorba and Bruce Alfonso de Bourbon-Condé, or simply Bruce Condé, and claimed to be descended from French royalty. However, the House of Bourbon-Condé had expired with the death of Prince Louis VI on August 27, 1830.[8] After the marriage, Chalmers adopted Brimeyer, who was afforded the pretext to add Bourbon-Condé to his name. Aside from being a royal imposter, Chalmers had severed as a major in the U.S. Army in Europe and Japan and, as an avid stamp collector from boyhood, persuaded the postal authorities of the oil-poor emirate of Sharjah to issue commemorative postage stamps of dubious philatelic value in order to generate revenue. His military background resulted in his appointment as a general of the Royalist forces during the North Yemen Civil War. Having renounced his American citizenship, Bruce Chalmers died of cancer, stateless, in Tangier on July 20, 1992.

---

[8] The prince was found "hanging" by the neck from the hasp of a window by a double handkerchief tied in a weaver's knot but his feet were touching the ground. Rumors of murder or suicide abounded, but it is likely the prince was using strangulation as a sexual stimulant. The practice is known as autoerotic asphyxiation or the choking game and is often fatal.

Brimeyer's final desperate attempt at ennobling himself occurred in the 1990's when two Serbian nationalists visited him in Spain and offered him the throne of Serbia after he had convinced them that he was descended from Hrebeljanović Nemanitch, the great-grandson of Czar Nicolas II. Brimeyer told journalists that he had been in touch with the then President of Serbia, Slobodan Milošević, supposedly in favor of restoring the Serbian monarchy, and claimed to have accepted the throne of Serbia. Alexis Brimeyer died of AIDS in Madrid in March 1995.

VI.

Article I of the Constitution of the United States prohibits both the states and the federal government from granting titles of nobility. Furthermore, Section 9 of Article I prohibits any person of noble title from holding any public office without the consent of Congress.

However, the Constitution does not ban American citizens from receiving titles of nobility from other countries. In fact, one of the countesses I knew in France was a colleague of mine, an American woman who had married a French count whose family was ennobled in the eighteenth century. Such titles are legitimate, whereas the Hoernle's titles were specious and illegitimate. Additionally, a proposed amendment to the American Constitution currently pending, states that if any citizen accepts a foreign title of nobility "such person shall cease to be a citizen of the United States."

Adolph and Henrietta Hoernle were harmless megalomaniacs, gullible victims of an unscrupulous huckster and convicted felon. The phony orders of chivalry to which they and their friends claimed allegiance were nothing more than pretexts to dress up and party. Ultimately, however, although their titles and their pretensions may have been bogus, the Hoernles' philanthropy was unequivocally genuine. Nevertheless, the Hoernles could have exercised just as much philanthropy if they had not claimed to be European nobility. Most wealthy philanthropists don't pretend to be counts or countesses, just as many authentic counts and countesses are poor as Job's turkey. Some find themselves burdened with dilapidated châteaux that cost too much to maintain or repair and are not noteworthy enough to merit subsidies from the French government. Many endeavor to marry off their sons to the daughters of titans of industry, thereby transforming the girls from mere commoners into countesses.

These impoverished noble families eke out their lives confined to cramped living quarters of just a few rooms, the others unoccupied. I visited one decrepit old château in Provence whose aristocratic owners had to share their home with a colony of bats. Others simply sell out to wealthy foreigners: the Château and picturesque garden of Betz in Picardy, originally built in the eighteenth century for Maria-Caterina Brignole, Princess of Monaco, now belong to the king of Morocco.

In France, the Association d'Entraide de la Noblesse Française, or ANF, was founded in 1932 in order to authenticate individuals who possess legitimate claim to the nobility and assist them whenever necessary. To date, the ANF has admitted only 2,666 families as members. Needless to say, neither "de Hoernle" nor "Bourbon-Condé" appears in its *Table de Familles*, which can be consulted on the ANF website.

On October 7, 2014, The South Florida *Sun-Sentinal* reported that more than 600 well-wishers sang "Happy Birthday" and gave the Lynn Philharmonia a standing ovation at Henrietta's 102th birthday concert in the Wold Performing Arts Center at Lynn University in Boca Raton. Because she had suffered a mild stroke and was unable to attend the event, her daughter Carol Wagman, of York, Pennsylvania, stood in for her. In an interview in the *Sun Sentinal* of March 18, 2015, Henrietta declared, "When you have money you should give it wisely. What good is your money when you're gone?"

On September 19, 2015, Henrietta not only appeared, but also spoke from the stage before more than 650 well-wishers and with humor before her 103rd birthday benefit concert. The Lynn Philharmonia under the direction of maestro Jon Robertson performed "A Knight [*sic*]in Budapest," a program of two Hungarian Dances by Brahms, the Gypsy Baron Overture by Strauss, the Hungarian Rhapsody No. 2 by Liszt and other pieces. Henrietta stated that she had chosen Hungarian music "because it's happy and exciting." *The Sun Sentinal* reported that "On their way out, people posed for selfies with a life-size cardboard cutout of the Countess in full regalia."

In retrospect, I'm sorry I missed the concert. After all, I needn't have spent $150 for a VIP Ticket, "including the 6:30 PM VIP Reception." I could have purchased a General Ticket for only $35.00. I could have rented black tie and declared myself a distant relative of Lloyd Tyrell-Kenyon, 6th Baron Kenyon, who is, decidedly, not a fake. What would they have cared?

VII.

On July 24, 2016, in an article by Staff Writer Sonja Isger, the *Palm Beach Post* reported that Henrietta Hoernle had died on the preceding Friday at the age of 103. She was survived her daughter Carol Wegman and another daughter, Diana Burgess, of New York City. Ironically, Wayne L. Ezell, who had co-authored the exposé of the Hoernles in 1992, died two days later near Glenwood, Iowa, at the age of 72, after a pickup truck ran into him on the first day of a week-long bicycling event. Isger's obituary quotes Ezell's defense of his story about the Hoernles, which he saw as "a commentary on so-called high society in our city."

Betty Mae Tiger Jumper, Isaac Hodgen Trabue and Wael Dubbaneh

I.

My brother and his wife invited me to spend a weekend with them at their home on the Gulf Coast of Florida, in Punta Gorda. All in all, 139 miles (223 km) separate West Palm Beach and Punta Gorda, and the two cities lie on almost the same latitude.

Only 11% of the land in the State of Florida is urbanized, leaving almost 90% of the land sparsely populated or uninhabited. To most Americans, "Florida" is synonymous with "the beach," and the vast majority of Floridians inhabit narrow strips of land close to the 825 miles (1,300 km) of beaches along the Atlantic and Gulf of Mexico coastlines.

Although most highways in Florida run north-south, State Highway 80 runs 123 miles (200 km) straight across central Florida from Palm Beach to Fort Myers. The first section was completed in 1924 in the West and it was extended to the Atlantic by 1945. In West Palm, State Route 80 bears the name

Southern Boulevard. Because of rapid urbanization west of the city, it became overcrowded, pockmarked with dangerous intersections and subject to increasing gridlock. Locals dubbed it "Killer 80" because of its high fatality rate. However, many upgrading and widening projects were undertaken early in the twenty-first century and construction continues. Florida State Route 80 even boasts its own website.

State Route 80 passes through a region known as the Florida Heartland. The history of the area comprises several phases, the first being settlement by Native Americans. The next phase was logging, one of whose purposes was to manufacture crossties for the railroad lines that crisscrossed Florida in the 1920's. Today, farming and cattle grazing are the primary economic activities in the Florida Heartland. Along with beef production, major crops are tomatoes, sugarcane, cucumbers and citrus. Only three main towns are located along the route, Belle Glade, Clewiston, and La Belle.

Belle Glade (population 18,000) was dubbed "Muck City" due to the large quantity of muddy soil in which sugarcane grows. About half the sugarcane in the United States is cultivated in the plains around Belle Glade and Clewiston.

Located on the southern shore of Lake Okeechobee, Clewiston (population 6,200) became known as "America's sweetest town" after sugarcane plantations were established in the area. Originally a Seminole fishing camp, the first permanent settlement began in 1920, when John O'Brien and Alonzo Clewis purchased a large tract of land and established a town.

The town of La Belle, nicknamed "the Belle of the Caloosahatchee," has a population of around 5,000 and was named for Belle Hendry, the daughter of pioneer cattleman Francis A. Hendry. In the nineteenth century the area was populated with cattle drovers and trappers. La Belle hosts an annual Swamp Cabbage Festival in February to commemorate Florida's state tree.

State Route 80 skirts the southern edge of Lake Okeechobee, the largest freshwater lake in Florida. "Big O" covers an area of 730 square miles (1,900 km²), but its average depth is only 9 feet (3 meters)!

II.

Not far west of Clewiston, on State Route 80, a sign on the south side of the highway points the way to the Big Cypress Seminole Reservation, located a little over 34 miles (54 km) to the south, the largest of six sections belonging to the Seminole Tribe of Florida. The land area is 82 square miles (212 km²), including the twelfth-largest cattle-raising operation in the United States, mostly free-range, grass-fed Angus raised for superior quality beef. This jet-black breed is particularly well-adapted to the hot and humid climate of central Florida.

Recent discoveries in a sinkhole in the Aucilla River, south of Tallahassee, indicate that the ancestors of today's Seminoles settled in what is now Florida as early as 14,500 years ago. Upon the arrival of the European colonists in the sixteenth century the indigenous population was an estimated 200,000. Devastated by conflicts and by diseases imported by the European intrusion, the survivors, along with runaway slaves, sought refuge in the vast interior.

As early as 1814, then Major General Andrew Jackson led an expedition against the Creek Indians. After defeating them, he then forced upon them a treaty whereby they surrendered to the United States over twenty-million acres of their traditional land in Alabama and Georgia. A forceful proponent of Indian removal, over the next decade, Jackson led the way in the campaign to drive Native Americans off their ancestral lands. The United States spent much of the first half of the nineteenth century attempting to dislodge about 5,000 Seminoles from Florida. In what is now known as the First Seminole War (1817-1818), Jackson caused an international furor when he led a force that invaded Spanish Florida, sacked and burned towns and seized Pensacola. After becoming president, he signed the Indian Removal act of 1830, enacted after fierce opposition in Congress, and launched a twenty-year program of ethnic cleansing, uprooting more than fifty thousand Cherokees, Chickasaws, Choctaws and Creeks and deporting them to the Indian Territory, now Oklahoma, where their descendants live today. A small group of Seminoles was coerced into signing the Treaty of Payne's Landing in 1832, agreeing to move west, but the majority of the tribe declared the treaty illegitimate and refused to leave. They defended themselves and their lands in the Second Seminole War (1835 to 1842), in which the United States Government squandered $40,000,000 rounding up 3,000 Seminole men, women and children like cattle and forcing them onto ships that transported them from Fort Brooke on Tampa Bay to New Orleans, then up the Mississippi to Fort Gibson in Arkansas, and from there into Oklahoma.

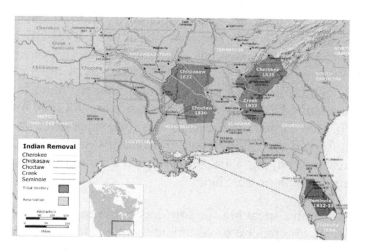

The Third Seminole War, consisting mostly of a number of skirmishes and incursions, took place from 1856 to 1858 and decimated the remainder of the tribe: most of the survivors capitulated and were shipped west. The hundred or so who sought refuge deep in the Everglades are the ancestors of today's Florida Seminoles. They are the only Native

American tribe that never signed a treaty of peace with the United States. Today more than 3,500 members of the tribe, referring to themselves as "the Unconquered," live on the six sections of their reservation. To document their history and heritage, they built the Ah-Tah-Thi-Ki Seminole Indian Museum in Big Cypress, housing over 30,000 archival items and artifacts.

Today, most conflicts involving Native Americans are waged against state governments over money: the tribes want to retain as much revenue as possible from their casinos, resorts, shopping malls and the sale of tax-free merchandise, and the states want to collect as much as possible in taxes from the tribes. Indians pay the same taxes as other citizens except that federal income taxes are not levied on income from trust lands held for them by the United States, state income taxes are not paid on income earned on a reservation, state sales taxes are not paid by Indians on transactions made on a reservation; and local property taxes are not paid on reservation or trust land.

Generally speaking, in conflicts between tribes and states, the federal government tends to side with the tribes owing to the special government-to-government relationship with them established in 1787 in Article I, Section 8 of the Constitution. It is under this provision that the government operates the Indian Health Service (IHS), an agency of the Department of Health and Human Services: Native

Americans, like veterans and those over 65, benefit from single-payer health insurance.[9]

By the mid-2000's, the Seminole Tribe of Florida was earning over $1 billion per year from gaming. In 2007 the tribe paid for $965 million to acquire Hard Rock International, a chain of themed Hard Rock Cafés, hotels and casinos in 45 countries, the first purchase of an international company by a Native American tribe. At a press conference in New York, Tribal Council member Max Osceola Jr. observed wryly, "Our ancestors sold Manhattan for trinkets. Today, with [this acquisition], we're going to buy Manhattan back one hamburger at a time."[10]

III.

The Seminoles also publish an informative monthly newspaper, the *Seminole Tribune*, originally known as *The Smoke Signal*, co-founded in 1956 by the remarkable Betty Mae Tiger Jumper (1923-2011), who overcame almost insuperable odds to become the first woman chief of any Native American nation.

Born the daughter of a Seminole mother, Ada Tiger, and a French trapper and sugarcane cutter, Abraham

---

[9] The IHS is severely under-funded and under-staffed; wealthy tribes like the Seminoles supplement or replace this service with their own clinics, hospitals and medical personnel.

[10] Cattelino, Jessica R., "One Hamburger at a Time: Revisiting the State-Society Divide with the Seminole Tribe of Florida and Hard Rock International" in *Current Anthropology*, Volume 52, Supplement 3, April 2011.

Barton, in a chickee[11] village near present-day Indiantown, in Martin County, Betty Mae Tiger and her brother risked death because tribal elders disliked mixed-race children, and often abandoned them in the Everglades to die. She related the incident in an interview with Dan McDonald of the *Seminole Tribune* when she was 74 years old: "I was a half-breed. An evil one. A group of men came to the camp and said that my brother and I must be destroyed or we would bring bad luck on the tribe." Her great-uncle Jimmie Gopher grabbed his rifle and fired shots at the men to chase them away. Afterwards, he moved Ada and her two children to Dania, a 497-acre tract of Seminole land in Broward County that would later be renamed the Hollywood Seminole Indian Reservation.

Young Betty Mae, who grew up speaking only the Miccosukee and Creek languages, decided she wanted to learn English after befriending another Native American girl while on a church-sponsored trip to Oklahoma. The girl was reading a comic book. "She told me the pictures talked to her. Talked to her. I was amazed. But I knew I had to learn the secret of reading." Astonishingly, at the time, Seminole children could not attend any of the segregated schools in Florida. As she put it, "The white schools wouldn't allow an Indian to enroll, so my mother thought I could go to school with the colored kids. But they wouldn't let me in either.

---

[11] A Seminole chickee, reproduced on the tribal logo, is an open structure consisting of palm or palmetto thatching on a log frame with a raised floor.

They said their schools were only for the colored. I was left out."

At the age of 14, she, her cousin and her brother succeeded in enrolling in a boarding school in Cherokee, North Carolina, operated by the Quakers, where she became the first Florida Seminole to learn to read and write English. She graduated from high school in 1945 and the following year completed nursing training at an IHS facility, the Kiowa Teaching Hospital in Lawton, Oklahoma. After returning to Florida, in 1946, she married Moses Jumper (1927-1992), a veteran of the U.S. Navy and a descendant of Chief Jumper, one of the last Seminole leaders to resist deportation during the Seminole Wars.

Betty Mae Tiger Jumper worked as a nurse for 40 years and was chosen to serve as Chairwoman of the Tribal Council of the Seminoles from 1967 to 1971. She was the author of three books; *A Seminole Legend,* her engrossing memoir written in collaboration with Patsy West, published in 2001; *And with the Wagon-Came God's Word* (2000), a history of the growth of Christianity among the Seminoles; and *Legends of the Seminole*s, a collection of ancestral stories and legends, published in 1994, the same year, she was inducted into the Florida Women's Hall of Fame. When Dan McDonald asked her in the interview what she missed most from the early days, Betty Mae replied, "The quiet. We used to sit outside and you could hear the hawks and owls and whippoorwills. We would sit around a camp fire and listen to the birds and frogs. The peaceful sounds. That was wonderful. That is what I miss the most. The quiet."

IV.

Arriving at Fort Myers on State Route 80, drivers can reach Punta Gorda on Interstate 75, a high-speed superhighway, or U.S. Route 41. Known as the Tamiami Trail, U.S. Route 41 was constructed in 1928 during the first Florida land boom to connect Tampa on the Gulf Coast with Miami on the Atlantic Ocean.

Punta Gorda, population around 17,000, is located 23 miles (37 km) north-northwest of Fort Myers on the south bank of the Peace River and the eastern shore of Charlotte Harbor, an arm of the Gulf of Mexico. In 1521, the Spanish conquistador Juan Ponce de León organized a colonizing expedition that is believed to have come ashore at a point within the Ponce de León Historical Park, a recreational area maintained by the city of Punta Gorda.[12] The settlers were met with resistance by the indigenous Calusa, and the conquistador was struck in the thigh by an arrow tipped with poisonous sap from the manchineel tree. The colonists were evacuated to Havana, Cuba, where Ponce de León died of his injury.

---

[12] There is also a Punta Gorda in Belize. *Punta gorda* means "fat point" in English and describes the broad arm of land jutting into a body of water. Grosse Pointe, Michigan, derives from the same term in French.

A permanent settlement was not established until the 1880's, long after Florida had been ceded to the United States by Spain in 1821 according to the Adams-Onis Treaty of 1819. The United States did not buy Florida, but absolved Spain of any claims made for damage caused by American citizens in Spanish West Florida with a five-million-dollar maximum limitation for these reparations.[13]

In the early 1880's a lawyer from Kentucky, Col. Isaac Hodgen Trabue, and his wife paid $1.25 an acre to acquire 30 acres of land around Charlotte Harbor with the intention of growing tropical fruits and raising cattle. In 1885 he laid out a plan for a town and named it Trabue, after himself. He gave the streets the names of his relatives and friends— Virginia, Olympia, Retta, Harvey, Gill—and created parks along the waterfront of Charlotte Harbor that exist to this day. In 1886, Trabue struck a deal with Henry Plant of the Southern Florida Railway for Plant to extend the narrow-gauge tracks from Arcadia to his town in exchange for 15 acres of land. The wood-burning locomotives pulled coaches carrying land developers and the first tourists to southwest Florida. Suddenly, the land was worth $3,000 an acre; a pretty fair return on a $1.25 investment. Trabue also made the area the leading producer of pineapples in the United States, but the pinery was wiped out in the freeze of 1917.

---

[13] Wasserman, Adam, *A People's History of Florida 1513-1876*, Third Edition, 2009, page 193.

Isaac Hodgen Trabue was born in Russell County, Kentucky on March 25, 1829. According to his biographers, his ancestors were French Huguenots, Protestants forced into exile after 1685 when Louis XIV, considering them heretics, forbade the practice of their religion, persecuted them and ordered them to renounce their faith and join the Catholic Church. Many sought refuge in America, where emigrants enjoyed religious freedom. Isaac Trabue was the descendant of Antoine Trabue (1667-1724); born in the southwest French city of Montauban, he escaped to Switzerland in 1687 and emigrated to Virginia in 1700. Trabue's wife Virginia was the daughter of Charlotte de Bernier Taylor (1806-1861), one of the world's first woman entomologists.

Isaac Trabue was educated in Georgetown, Kentucky and graduated in law from Transylvania University in Lexington. The 1904-1905 edition of the *Encyclopedia Americana* states that "at the outbreak of the Civil War he recruited a company for the Union army and served through the war as captain and as colonel," and *Men of the Century,* published in 1896, reports that he "espoused the cause of the Union and helped turn the tide of Kentucky's neutrality for the Union." However, an obituary published in the *Frankfort Roundabout* of July 20, 1907, states that Col. Trabue was "the brave and gallant commander of the Second Kentucky Regiment, Confederate States Army," and the *Library of Southern Literature*, from 1907, also affirms that Trabue served in the Confederate Army. It would appear that these writers erroneously attributed Trabue's loyalties, whether by accident or intentionally.

Col Trabue sent his female slaves to work as nurses in military hospitals and his male slaves to the quartermaster's corps. After the Civil War, Col. Trabue became involved in Kentucky politics: he was the Republican candidate for Congress in 1872, and in 1877 and 1879 he ran for state offices on the Greenback Party ticket, but he never won an election.

In 1880, a group of 34 men met at Tom Hector's Billiard Parlor and Drugstore and incorporated the town as Punta Gorda, the name given to the area by the Spanish navigators. Col. Trabue was furious and, after the election of Republican President Benjamin Harrison, Trabue, one of the few Republicans in the state, succeeded in obtaining a presidential appointment as postmaster of Punta Gorda for Robert Meacham, the biracial son of a slave mother and her white master, State Senator Banks Meacham, who home-schooled his son. This time, Trabue's enemies—the Democrats—were furious. Robert Meacham, born in 1835, had helped establish the African Methodist Episcopal Church in Florida and become active in Florida politics during Reconstruction, participating in the drafting of the Florida Constitution of 1868 that guaranteed ex-slaves the right to vote and hold office. He was elected to the Florida Senate in 1877 and died in 1902.

Isaac Trabue was a recognized chess master who defeated World Champion Johannes Zukertort in a match in 1883 in Louisville and allocated some of the proceeds of his pineapple plantation to pay for the gold medals at the annual chess tournaments he sponsored. In 1904 he developed and published a method for four players to play chess. He also published a drama with the unlikely title of *Hobson Blowing up the Merrimack in Santiago Bay,* inspired by an episode of the Spanish-American War and, in 1900, he published under the pseudonym "Captain Puntagorda," a satirical novel entitled *Black Wench.*

In 1907, old, infirm and embittered, Isaac Trabue took his wife and moved back to Kentucky, where he died on July 16, leaving an estate valued at $500,000. He is buried in the cemetery in Frankfort. Virginia returned to Punta Gorda; she died in 1924 and is buried in Indian Springs Cemetery. Today, the only monument to Col. Isaac Hodgen Trabue in Punta Gorda is an upscale restaurant named in his honor.

V.

On my last evening in Punta Gorda, we took the Tamiami Trail across the bridge to Port Charlotte where we had dinner at one of the most famous local eateries, Wally's Southern Style BBQ. Barbecue—also spelled BBQ—is found all over the United States, but is a particular tradition in the South. It is a method in which meat is cooked at low temperatures for long periods of time—often up to 24 hours—over indirect heat from cookers fired by wood or charcoal that generate aromatic smoke and in which the flames do not contact the meat directly as in grilling. Each locality has its variety of barbecue, particularly the recipe for the sauce, and chefs endeavor to outperform their rivals. Barbecue competitions are conducted all over the United States, the most famous being the annual World Championship Barbecue Cooking Contest held in Memphis, Tennessee.

Wally's somewhat disconcerting slogan, posted prominently on his website proclaims: "So tender, U' Need No Teeth to Eat This Meat." Owner-chef Wael Dubbaneh is a graduate of Le Cordon Bleu in Orlando; he appends "CC" to his name on his business card to indicate his membership in the Chefs Collaborative, a non-profit association founded by a group of visionary chefs including Nora Pouillon, who opened America's first organic restaurant in Washington, and Alice Waters, the owner of Chez Panisse in Berkeley and prominent in the Slow Food movement supporting small farmers, healthy food, and sustainable agriculture.

Having lived and worked in the Middle East and written about Bahrain and its neighbor Saudi Arabia, I knew that with a name like "Wael," he had to be an Arab and concluded that he had Americanized his name to "Wally" to make it easier to pronounce. When the maître d' arrived to seat us, he looked as if he had just arrived from the Levant. "Are you Wael?" I asked him. "No, I'm not." Then he disappeared into the kitchen. If it wasn't Wael himself, it must have been a relative.

According to a review of his restaurant, Dubbaneh was born and raised in Jordan. He is one of the estimated 75,000 members of the Antiochian Orthodox Christian church in North America; on his Facebook page, he cites the Bible as his favorite book. Ten to twelve million Arabs are Christian, living mostly in Egypt, Lebanon and Syria.

Wally's offers BBQ made from fresh pork, beef, and chicken, slow cooked in the smoker on the premises. Wally's recipe resembles the Kentucky variety: the meat is rubbed with dry seasoning and cooked without sauce in a smoker fired with hickory; the sauce is served on the side. We ordered platters of pulled pork accompanied by copious portions of various side dishes, including fries made from sweet potatoes. The term "pulled meat" refers to cuts barbecued at low temperatures and smoked in a slow cooker until the meat pulls easily from the bone. It was all quite delicious—authentic American cuisine. If friends from France were visiting me, I would take them to Wally's.

Needless to say, Wally—or Wael—knows what he is doing. Out of 333 reviews of Wally's on TripAdvisor.com, 152 rated it "excellent" and 125 "very good." TripAdvisor awarded Wally's its Certificate of Excellence in 2013, and readers of the *Charlotte Sun* voted it "number one ribs and barbecue" each year for many years.

VII.

Betty Mae Tiger Jumper was a Native American who was not even allowed to attend school as a child. Col. Isaac Trabue was the descendant of French Huguenots, persecuted in their homeland. Wael Dubbanel is a Christian who left his home in a predominantly Muslim country to seek his fortune in America. Despite the hardships each of them or their forebears underwent, their individual success stories testify to the reality of the American Melting Pot and the possibilities for anyone to succeed, no matter what his or her origin.

"I was an FBI slave."

I.

Like most of the Floridians in this book, Carroll Hubbard Jr. was a transplant. He was not a billionaire splitting his time between an estate in the Hamptons and a mansion on Palm Beach Island. And he wasn't one of the snowbirds from Québec, migrating to spend exactly 120 days in the United States in order not to lose their generous single-payer Canadian health insurance. Nor was he a college student invading Florida for a Spring Break of hooking up and binge drinking. Carroll's all-expenses-paid sojourn in the Sunshine State lasted from 1995 to 1997. He was not on vacation, but a guest of the United States taxpayer, incarcerated in the Eglin Federal Prison Camp near Fort Walton Beach.

Although Carroll was born in Murray, Kentucky, he spent much of his childhood in Ashland, Kentucky, where his father was the minister of the First Baptist Church. Carroll's younger brother Kyle was a classmate of mine in elementary school. Although I was a Methodist, my parents overcame their diffidence and allowed me to accept Kyle's invitation to attend the Baptists' summer Bible School, and we often had play dates in each other's homes. Our paths separated, first when Kyle and I attended separate high schools, then when Reverend Hubbard was transferred to another church. I did not see Carroll again for another thirty years.

II.

Instead of following his father's footsteps into the ministry, Carroll decided to serve the people on a practical, rather than a spiritual plane, by going into politics. After graduating from Georgetown College, a private, liberal-arts institution in Georgetown, Kentucky, whose history dates back to 1787, He obtained a Juris Doctor degree from the University of Louisville Law School in 1962 and began a life-long political career by running successfully for the Kentucky State Senate where he served from 1968 through 1974.

On January 2, 1974, Carroll, then 36 years old, announced his candidacy for the U.S. House of Representatives for the First District of Kentucky. In his announcement he criticized "nonproductive, inactive elected officers," making pointed criticisms of the important votes missed by the incumbent congressman, Frank Stubblefield, who had left Washington to campaign back in Kentucky.

In what could have passed for a sermon, Carroll explained why he had switched in his senior year from studying for the ministry to pursuing a career in law and government, citing 2 Chronicles 7:14 as his inspiration: "...our problems are not just political and economic but indeed are also spiritual and moral. We need a return to God's standards of decency and integrity." The *Kentucky New Era* accompanied its story with a photograph of Carroll with his wife, the former Joyce Lynn Hall of Metropolis, Illinois, and their two young daughters.

In a stunning upset victory, Carroll defeated Stubblefield and went on to win the seat in Congress, where he was chosen by his peers as president of the House freshman class of 1974, composed of 75 Democrats and only 17 Republicans. The Democrats became known as "Watergate Babies."

Carroll was reëlected to Congress another eight times, serving a total of eighteen years, from January 3, 1975, to January 3, 1993. An analysis of the bills he sponsored and cosponsored in 1992 reveals him to be firmly in the center of the political spectrum, an independent voice between Democrats and Republicans, although far below average on the "leadership" scale. Ironically, given future events, a third of the bills he sponsored were in the category of Crime and Law Enforcement.

Carroll's campaigns were so successful that, on at least one occasion, he ran unopposed in the Democratic primary. One of the secrets of Carroll's success was pointed out in an article in the December 12, 1993, issue of the *New York Times*: "[Carroll] was best known for tending to local concerns of his district in western Kentucky." Along with that, Carroll, like Lyndon Johnson, another Southerner whose sense of inferiority he shared, possessed an almost photographic memory for his constituents' names and the details of their lives.

III.

How did I end up working for Carroll, with whom I had had no contact whatsoever since we were children? As is often the case, I got the job by pure serendipity. I had been living in Paris and wanted to spend Christmas of 1982 with my mother and brother in Kentucky. On my way, I stopped over in Washington. Remembering that Carroll was a member of Congress, I simply went up to the Hill, located his office in the Rayburn Building, walked in, introduced myself, and handed my card (with my Paris address) to Betty Wood, the receptionist, who then left her desk to go into Carroll's office. A few moments later the solid oak door blew open as if by a hurricane and Carroll strode out, stocky and rubicund, with his right arm stretched out to envelop my hand. As he propelled me into the inner sanctum, he asked imperiously, "Have you called your mother?" It wasn't a question, but an accusation. I realized that with his stentorian voice he could just as easily have been an evangelist humiliating a sinner: "Have you taken Jesus Christ as your savior?" The Church had never left Carroll. "No, I haven't," I replied sheepishly. "Then get on that phone and call her up right now," he commanded. It is easy to imagine my mother's astonishment when I told her I was sitting in Congressman Carroll Hubbard's office!

At that time, Carroll was Chairman of the Subcommittee on Panama Canal/Outer Continental Shelf. During our conversation, I learned that there was an opening on the subcommittee staff and Carroll learned that I not only was knowledgeable in Spanish, having studied Latin American language and literature at the University of Michigan with the eminent Argentine writer and critic, Enrique Anderson-Imbert, but that I had also worked for seven years for Total, the French oil and natural gas conglomerate, during which time I had served on a mission to the petroleum producing region of Hassi Messaoud in Algeria. Without even knowing it, I found myself possessing the background and qualifications that suited me to serve on Carroll's subcommittee. I held the position of investigative researcher for the next two years.[14]

---

[14] After the Republican takeover of the House in 1995, the subcommittee, along with its parent, the Committee on Merchant Marine and Fisheries, was abolished and its jurisdiction assigned to other committees.

Carroll was not the easiest boss to work for, and he often made the list of the worst bosses on Capitol Hill, compiled annually by one of the local journals. Since these were not civil service positions, any staffer could be terminated at any time: one young woman, fresh out of law school, lost her job as subcommittee counsel after a couple of weeks because she answered a phone call from a reporter of the Louisville *Courier-Journal*, unaware that all calls from the media had to be forwarded to the press secretary. Another short-timer, Richard Paul, left Carroll's employ for a job as a Senate staffer. In 1985, joined a political satire troupe, the Capitol Steps and, later, became a radio producer. One new hire only lasted half a day: she found the work environment so unnerving that she never returned from her lunch break.

In those days, we didn't have computers, but pounded out enormous amounts of official correspondence each day on IBM Selectric typewriters. The deafening racket of half a dozen of these machines clattering at once made the office sound like a foundry. And what about backup copies of this voluminous correspondence? Deprived of computers, we used carbon paper and retained the copies in three-ring binders. And what is carbon paper? Invented in 1801, it's a sheet coated on one side with a layer of pigmented ink bound with montan wax; a sheet of carbon paper is sandwiched between the original and a blank piece of paper. The ink stains your fingers, and if you make a typing mistake...well, you don't want to make any typing mistakes.

Every member of the staff dreaded the convocation of a "staff meeting." Instead of being an occasion for a give-and-take between Carroll and his aides, it resembled kangaroo court or a trial under the Spanish Inquisition, with Carroll as Torquemada. He was a stickler for correct spelling, a characteristic he had certainly acquired from his schoolteacher mother, and he took perverse delight in humiliating a staffer who had committed the cardinal sin of misspelling a word. Carroll would hold up a letter written by the offender and excruciatingly rip it down the middle. I'll never forget that sound: it was if the staffer's soul was being torn in half. Nevertheless, staff turnover was not particularly high since Carroll compensated his employees with very generous salaries.

In those years, I learned about Washington politics from the inside, which complimented the theory I had learned in my political science classes. We scheduled legislative and oversight hearings, contacted witnesses and prepared briefing books for the chairman and the other members of the subcommittee. We held field hearings on offshore oil and gas issues in Santa Barbara, California, and in New Orleans and Houma, Louisiana, where we also were flown by helicopter to offshore platforms to inspect safety measures designed to protect the crew. During the hearings in Louisiana in 1983, numerous witnesses testified that the existent levee system was woefully inadequate and that, sooner or later, New Orleans would be inundated. The warnings were ignored, the necessary funds were never allocated and the dire predictions came true when Hurricane Katrina devastated New Orleans in August 2005, resulting in the death of over 1,500 people in Louisiana alone and total damage estimated at over $100 billion.

I also accompanied Carroll and other subcommittee members and staff in a Congressional Delegation (known in Pentagonese as a CODEL), in which we visited Panama as part of our oversight jurisdiction over the Panama Canal. In addition to attending meetings, some of us were taken on several adventures including boarding a cargo ship as it was transiting the canal and a thrilling helicopter flight down the twists and turns of the Chagres River through a pristine rainforest to the Caribbean Sea.

Panama is one of the few countries in the world without its own paper money. [15] Instead, the United States dollar is the sole legal tender in the country, but Panamanian refer to the banknotes as "balboas," named for Vasco Núñez de Balboa, the conquistador who crossed the isthmus to the Pacific in 1513. Dollars that aren't called dollars can be disconcerting to visitors, but not to money

---

[15] Balboa banknotes were issued on October 2, 1941, under President Arnulfo Arias. A week later, he was overthrown in a coup and the bills were withdrawn and incinerated, giving them the name "Seven Day Balboas." Panama issues coins of 1 and 5 centésimos and $\frac{1}{10}$, $\frac{1}{4}$, and $\frac{1}{2}$ balboa, the same weight, dimensions, and composition as similar American coins.

launderers: as soon as an attaché case crammed with $1.2 million in bundles of hundred-dollar bills arrives in Panama, its contents are transmuted as if by magic into balboas. Dollars become balboas, so they aren't dollars any more: it's monetary legerdemain. This fact goes a long way to explain the number of skyscrapers in Panama City, making it resemble a miniature Manhattan. The 11.5 million Panama Papers, released in 2016, provide many insights into how Panamanian shell corporations were used for fraud, kleptocracy, tax evasion and evading international sanctions.

IV.

On September 1, 1983, Carroll narrowly cheated death. He had been invited with two senators, Republicans Jesse Helms of North Carolina and Steve Symms of Idaho, along with Democratic Congressman Larry McDonald of Georgia, to attend the celebration in Seoul of the thirtieth anniversary of the U.S.-South Korea Mutual Defense Treaty. Although the four had originally planned to take the same flight, delays in connecting flights to JFK Airport resulted in Symms taking one flight, and Helms and Carroll planning to join McDonald on a later flight. As the delays mounted, instead of joining McDonald, Carroll canceled his reservation and accepted a speaking engagement in Kentucky. McDonald boarded Korean Air Lines flight KAL 007 on August 31 and Helms flew on yet another flight.

For reasons that remain fully unexplained, on September 1, 1983, KAL 007 deviated from its assigned flight path over Japan and veered 300 miles off course into prohibited Soviet airspace over Sakhalin Island. At around the same time, a United States Air Force RC-135 reconnaissance aircraft was flying in the area, preparing to monitor a Soviet missile test scheduled for the same day. KAL 007 was shot down by a Sukhoi Su-15 interceptor and all 269 people aboard, including 63 Americans, died. In the aftermath, U.S.-Soviet relations, which were already tense during the Cold War, deteriorated, and the unanswered questions about the shootdown resulted in much controversy and gave birth to numerous conspiracy theories. In an extensive interview with *New York Times* reporter Michael R. Gordon in December 1996, Gennadi Osipovich, the Sukhoi pilot, still maintained that the aircraft was on a spying mission.

V.

During his 18-year congressional career, Carroll had two brushes with the law; he won the first case, but lost the second. According to the Constitution, the system of checks and balances sets clear limits on the power of each of the three branches of government, but the authors of the Constitution expected the greater power to lie with Congress. For example, the president nominates justices to the Supreme Court, but they must be approved by a majority of the Senate.

The Constitution also gives Congress the authority to organize the Supreme Court, allowing legislators to increase or decrease the number of justices as they see fit. Over the years, the number has varied from five to ten; the current number of nine Supreme Court justices was set in 1869.

Normally, the Executive Branch does not interfere in the workings of Legislative Branch since each house has its ethics committee empowered to recommend censure and expulsion of a member for misconduct. However, the FBI has occasionally conducted an investigation into alleged congressional misbehavior, the most notable being the Abscam operation in the late 1970's in which six members of the House and one senator were convicted of bribery and conspiracy: most resigned and one was expelled.

Carroll came under the scrutiny of the Department of Justice in the early 1980's when it was alleged that he used some of his aides to perform campaign chores. After two years, the FBI investigators came up empty-handed, the inquiry was closed and the department's Public Integrity Section declined to prosecute. The procedure might not have been undertaken if the investigators had studied the House Ethics Manual, whose rules state clearly and unambiguously that staff members can be assigned to work on campaign matters after they have completed their official duties for the day. Carroll was only one of many who engaged in this practice. He was investigated; they weren't.

Investigative journalist Jack Anderson devoted his column of March 21, 1985, to this case, in which he described Carroll as a "a victim" and quoted Carroll as stating, "You have no idea how I've suffered, and what I've been through."

VI.

A candidate in the Democratic primary of 1992, Carroll lost the race to Thomas Jefferson Barlow, receiving 37,188 votes to Barlow's 40,014. Barlow was subsequently elected, but lost his bid for reëlection in 1994, one of many victims of the Republican sweep to power in which they gained control of both the Senate and the House for the first time in 40 years.

The reason for Carroll's surprising loss in the 1992 primary and his subsequent trial, conviction and incarceration are the direct consequences of a daring and unconventional scheme that Carroll concocted, unprecedented in the annals of American political history. It is also a drama that is largely unknown to the general public, even to many Kentuckians.

In September 1983, Carroll and Joyce were divorced. According to a spokeswoman, the separation was "amicable and uncontested." Carroll then married Carol Fairchild Brown, a teacher from the eastern Kentucky town of Whitesburg, in 1984. She had won the title of Miss Kentucky in 1959, and was a divorcee with three daughters. The couple were now known as Carroll and Carol, and since the names are homonymous, it was easy to confuse one with the other.

After serving so long in Congress, Carroll harbored a dream of running for governor of Kentucky and after that, perhaps, capping his career with a term in the United States Senate. Although well-known in western Kentucky, he had little name recognition in the eastern part of the state. It was thus that Carroll hatched a daring if unconventional scheme for Carol Fairchild Brown Hubbard to run as a candidate in the Democratic primary for the seat of the Fifth District of Kentucky in 1992. A headline in the *Washington Post* of November 27, 1990, summed it up concisely: "Kentucky Delegation May Get 2nd Hubbard." The article, by columnist David S. Broder, continued: "The Kentucky congressional delegation in 1993 could face an identity crisis unknown in the annals of Capitol Hill...Should [Carol Fairchild Brown] and her husband both win seats, they would form the first husband-and-wife team from the same state in the history of Congress."

Carol received a total of $114,282 in campaign contributions, mostly from Kentucky law firms and banks. Despite this war chest and the assistance of her husband, for which she would later pay a heavy price, Carol placed a dismal third in a field of six candidates, thereby ending her short-lived political career.

As for Carroll, he was accused of assigning some of the staffers from his district offices in western Kentucky to work on his wife's campaign while they were still on the government payroll and transferring funds to her campaign from the account of his own campaign committee. Carroll was also accused of staging a Watergate-style burglary of his district office in Paducah in an attempt to destroy incriminating documents. If substantiated, these charges were violations of the law. Carroll and Carol Fairchild Brown would subsequently be tried and convicted for these charges.

Like Lyndon Johnson, Carroll always saw himself mistreated and maligned by the media, in Carroll's case, by his arch-enemy, the Louisville *Courier-Journal*. But On December 11, 1993, Carroll achieved one of his longtime goals by appearing on the front page of the *Washington Post*. That newspaper and the *New York Times* broke the story that Carroll had worked as an informer for the FBI using the alias "Elmer Fudd" for about six months in order to stave off prosecution and lighten the charges against him. According to the *Post*, "It is common for the [FBI] to use suspects as informers to help uncover crimes. In such cases, the Government typically promises that if a suspect is convicted, Federal prosecutors will recommend a reduced sentence in return for the suspect's coöperation." The *Post* quoted Carroll as saying, "For more than six months, I was an FBI slave." He stated that he wore a recorder and taped telephone conversations, believing that he was going to help the United States Government investigate Libya and Libyan lobbyists but, instead, according to the *Post*, he was used to gather information on local officials in Kentucky. Nonetheless, the *Times* quoted Dennis Null, a friend and former law partner, who maintained that Carroll had "traveled to Libya and met with the Libyan leader, Col. Muammar el-Qaddafi, in the course of his work as an informer."

Although it was indicated in some media accounts that Carroll had become entangled in the House Banking Scandal, he was not one of the 22 members of the House singled out by the House Ethics Committee for leaving their checking accounts overdrawn for over eight months. In reality, the scandal, nicknamed "Rubbergate" in an effort to mislead the public into believing that the checks had bounced, was a tempest in a teapot, mostly engineered by Republicans (only three of whom were among the 22). The "House Bank" was, in essence, merely a clearinghouse operated by the Sergeant at Arms as a courtesy to Members of Congress.[16] The rules of the House permitted its members to briefly overdraw their accounts without paying a penalty. Checks did not bounce; they were honored because the bank provided overdraft protection to its account holders. In essence, the House Bank was providing "payday loans" to Members of Congress without charging interest or

---

[16] The Sergeant at Arms has been elected at the beginning of each Congress since 1798 and is the chief law enforcement officer of the House, responsible for security, law enforcement and protocol.

service fees. The fact that Carroll admitted to having written 152 overdrafts was used to his advantage by Barlow, who had lost to Carroll by a 4-to-1 margin in the 1986 primary. Carroll attributed his defeat in the 1992 primary to "an anti-Washington sentiment across the country," but Barlow claimed that "The checks are just the straw that broke the camel's back."

The scandal resulted in the closure of the House Bank and the resignation under bipartisan pressure of Jack Russ, the Sergeant at Arms, whose office operated the facility.[17]

Carroll was convicted of three felony charges of violating federal campaign spending rules, conversion of federal property, theft and obstruction of justice and was sentenced to three years' imprisonment and a fine of $153,794. He began serving his sentence as Inmate #19595-016 on December 29, 1994, in the Federal Medical Center in Fort Worth, Texas, but shortly thereafter became a Floridian when he was transferred to the Federal Prison Camp at Eglin Air Force Base near Fort Walton Beach, one of 27 federal work camps where the U.S. Bureau of Prisons then housed its least dangerous felons.

Strat Douthat described the facility in the *Los Angeles Times* of April 23, 1989: "Deep in the aromatic pine woods of the Florida Panhandle is a small place where some of the best known and

---

[17] Members of the House, their families and their staff are entitled to open accounts in a full-service financial institution, the Congressional Federal Credit Union.

wealthiest of men come to spend time…Here these big shots may try Italian lawn-bowling or indulge themselves on the tennis courts, play a game of racquetball or take a turn on the foot trail that winds through the landscaped grounds and past a lake. In the evening guests can catch a movie on cable TV or, if they have money, visit the commissary for a cup of cappuccino and some Haagen-Dazs Macadamia Brittle." And Lacy Rose wrote in *Forbes* that Eglin was considered so cushy that the term "Club Fed" was coined to describe it. While Carroll was a Floridian, I maintained a correspondence with him, the only member of his staff to do so. Since he was not permitted to subscribe to certain periodicals but liked to keep abreast of events in Washington, I sent him copies of *Roll Call*, "the newspaper of Capitol Hill since 1955," hoping they would not be confiscated.

Douthat described the camp's drawbacks: "There is no swimming pool. And…everyone must sleep in a dormitory and work eight hours a day at a beginning pay rate of 11 cents an hour." He quoted inmates saying that the camp was "more hell than heaven." One of them complained, "The only thing this place is good for is to cause divorces and put children on the street without a father." Indeed, this was the case for Carroll: Carol Fairchild Brown filed for divorce in 1998.

Carroll was released from custody on July 22, 1997. The Eglin Federal Prison Camp was closed in February 2006 in a cost-cutting measure and its prisoners transferred to the camp at Pensacola.

For her part, Carol Brown Hubbard was sentenced on June 30, 1994, to five years of probation for aiding the theft of government property and ordered to perform 100 hours of community service and pay $27,000 in restitution. She had pleaded guilty in April to one misdemeanor count of aiding and abetting theft of government property after being accused of using her husband's congressional staffers on her failed campaign for the House in 1992.

I often spoke with Carol in Carroll's office during 1987, when the couple would attend receptions on Capitol Hill, and considered her a sweet Kentucky girl who had a lot of political acumen and never failed to charm those she met. I regretted that she was caught up in a maelstrom not of her making. She died on October 17, 2015, at the age of 75.

VII.

Imagine for a moment that Carol Fairchild Brown Hubbard had won the primary and had gone on to win a seat in Congress from the Fifth District and that Carroll Hubbard Jr. had been reëlected to represent the First District for a tenth term. For the first time in American history, both husband and wife, Carroll and Carol, would have been representing the same state in the House of Representatives. As Carol observed to David S. Broder, "I guess Carroll and I could drive to work together and home at the end of the day. Weekends, he'd go west and I'd go east." But this was not to pass.

VIII.   .

After serving two years and twenty days in prison, five months in a halfway house in Paducah, Kentucky, and one month of home incarceration in Mayfield, Kentucky, Carroll was employed by Paducah Medical Supply Inc., and hosted a weekly political radio show. On June 21, 1998, Carroll married his third wife, Vivian A. Taylor of Eddyville, Kentucky, who had been a campaign supporter. Always a ladies' man, he declared to *Roll Call* in its issue of July 20, 1998, "I'm thrilled to be in western Kentucky, happily married to a beautiful young blonde."

In 2001, Carroll brought a lawsuit in the Commonwealth of Kentucky Supreme Court against the Kentucky Bar Association in an effort to regain his license to practice law.

During the proceeding, Carroll admitted that the purpose of his conspiracy was to solidify support for him across the state in his quest to run for governor. He testified that his acts were foolish and that his judgment was clouded by arrogance and pride. He appreciated that his conduct was wrong, that what he did was a crime and devastating to his life and family. Kyle testified that his brother recognized the seriousness of what happened and was contrite. Most significantly, Kyle stated that, "It was the circumstances of raising two children and a second wife, who had three daughters, which caused [Carroll] to live above his means, but it was not what he wanted to do." In fact, by my reckoning, at the time of his misconduct, Carroll was the sole or principal support of eight women: in addition to his second wife and three daughters, I counted his elderly mother and his first wife and her two daughters.

In a controversial decision, Carroll won the case, and the Court granted his application to be reinstated to the practice of law on October 25, 2001. He thereafter founded a law office in Paducah, specializing in criminal defense cases.

After the death of his mother, Addie Shelton "Sarah" Hubbard, who died on January 12, 2005, at the age of 92, Carroll, ever the politician, returned to square one and attempted a political comeback by running for the Kentucky State Senate as he had back in 1968.

Two campaigns, in 2006 and 2008, were unsuccessful; although in the 2006 race he lost by a heartbreaking 58 votes. Undaunted, in 2012, he ran for Kentucky State Senate once more. Although unopposed in the Democratic primary, he lost to Republican Stan Humphries in the general election on November 6, 2012. Carroll Hubbard Jr.'s political career had finally come to an end.

Videos of 144 of Carroll's appearances in the House of Representatives can be consulted on C-Span.[18]

---

[18] http://www.c-span.org/person/?carrollhubbard

Of particular note is an eleven-minute interview he granted on October 6, 1992, in which he discusses his career on Capitol Hill. His remarks lamenting congressional gridlock and criticizing unchecked spending could easily have been delivered in 2016.

The Real Story of Carroll Hubbard Jr. incorporates all the elements of a Greek tragedy or a Christian morality play. His is the saga a good man laid low by vanity and arrogance and redeemed by confession and repentance.

Shopping for a Sportscoat

Sometimes, when I am in a particularly dyspeptic or dystopian mood, I despair over the thought that the principal economic activity of the United States consists of low-paid American wage-slaves peddling consumer goods manufactured by even lower-paid wage slaves toiling in the sweat-shops of South Asia and Central America. They live in countries like Vietnam, the grandchildren of the Viet Cong that Americans were annihilating with carpet bombing, napalm and Agent Orange only 50 years ago. Some live in Bangladesh, where at least 1,127 young women, who were being paid barely a dollar a day to sew clothes for gigantic American multinational corporations known to everyone, were killed when their factory collapsed on April 24, 2013. At the apex of the pyramid are, of course, the plutocrats, both American and foreign, who collect colossal salaries and obscene bonuses from this modern, globalized exploitation that could best be described as contemporary feudalism.

But it's not just the plutocrats who benefit from the system. Sometimes, the shoppers can benefit, too. Since I was in sunny Florida, I wanted to buy a light-weight blue jacket to wear to the training classes I was conducting at the time, so I went to

The Mall at Wellington Green, an upscale shopping plaza, to find the C. H. Parsons store.

The Mall at Wellington Green, built in 2001, is located in Wellington, on the edge of the Everglades, adjacent to the city of West Palm Beach. Wellington occupies what was originally the world's largest strawberry planation. According to the Wikipedia, the land was originally known as the Flying Cow Ranch; "Flying" because the founder was an aviator, and "Cow," an acronym of the initials for Charles Oliver Wellington who, in the 1950s, bought 18,000 acres (73 km^2) of land, which would eventually be reborn as the Village of Wellington. Like Juan Banús and Isaac Trabue, discussed elsewhere in this book, he named the town after himself.

As mentioned in a previous chapter, Wellington has developed into an international center for equestrian sports. In an article entitled, "Florida Town Where Wealthy Equine Enthusiasts Saddle Up," The *Wall Street Journal* reported on June 21, 2013, that "Wellington may be one of the few places in the world where it is possible to get a pickup game of polo...It has some 60 full-size polo fields and three polo clubs."

New York City is the home of 70 billionaires and many thousands of multi-millionaires, many if not most of whom are social parasites who never did an honest day's work in their entire lives but either inherited their wealth from their forebears or, like modern Rumpelstiltskins, spun gold from the straw of derivatives and credit default swaps or by rigging the stock market by using high-frequency trading to front-run orders placed by investors at no risk to themselves. It's the perfect investment, if not the perfect crime.[19] Strangely, however, many of these parasitic and peripatetic plutocrats claim Florida as their domicile. The reason: no personal income taxes are levied in the Sunshine State. By judiciously spending part of the year in New York and part in Florida, the super-rich can avoid paying the onerous New York state income taxes on their ill-gotten gains. It's not tax fraud, it's tax avoidance, and it's all perfectly legal. We poor schmucks pick up the tab for what the plutocrats don't want to pay.

The favorite perching place for the super-rich is Palm Beach, a town occupying most of a narrow, 26-mile long barrier island stretching between the Atlantic Ocean and the Intracoastal Waterway and connected to the mainland by several bridges. During the winter, known locally as "The Season," it is the home of the rich-and-famous and the rich-and-not-so-famous. The year-round population of Palm Beach is around 8,600, but can triple during The Season. Since Palm Beach borders the Atlantic, the entire town must be evacuated when threatened by a hurricane. Consequently, the billionaires simply board up their mansions and condominiums and migrate north to their summer quarters in the Hamptons or Newport well before Hurricane

---

[19] For the details, see the 2014 best-seller, *Flash Boys*, by Michael Lewis.

Season, which extends from June 1 through November 31, only to return, like migratory wildfowl, to winter in the tax-free Florida sunshine.

The town of Palm Beach is known in local parlance as "The Island." West Palm Beach, known to all as "West Palm," with a population of a little over 100,000, is the largest city in Palm Beach County and is located on the other side—snobs say the undesirable side—of the Intracoastal Waterway, which must be pronounced "Innercoastal." Seven other municipalities in the county attempt to capitalize on the glory, glitz and glamour of the magic name: There's North Palm Beach and South Palm Beach. (There is no East Palm Beach: it's the Atlantic Ocean.) For those who like water, there's Palm Beach Lakes and Palm Beach Shores. Those with a green thumb might prefer Palm Beach Gardens. There's even a Royal Palm Beach, where plebeians are presumably not welcomed except as serfs.

In April 2016, *Palm Beach Post* Staff Writer Frank Cerabino courageously—or recklessly—rated all 38 incorporated municipalities in Palm Beach County from worst to best, including descriptions of the municipal logo, a random factoid and a reason for ranking each choice.[20] Some towns bear unlikely names such as Briney Breezes (5th best) Pahokee (#37) and Hypoluxo (#29), the origin of whose

---

[20] Cerabino, Frank, "Ranking Palm Beach County's cities, from worst to best," *Palm Beach Post*, April 6, 2016.

name is disputed. Some say it derives from the Greek root *hypo-* (under, below average) and the Latin *lux* (light). It is possible the name comes from a loose translation of the Seminole name for Lake Worth, "water all around; I can't get out." I recommend that the town change its name to Hyperluxo: then people might think that it's a hyper-luxurious place to live and real-estate values would increase. The town of Golf (#19) probably include caddies in its population of 260. Homesick Californians will find Palm Springs (#31). And if you are looking for the lost city of Atlantis, it's in Palm Beach County—number 26. Now you know. As for Wellington (#4), I would suggest that it be dubbed "Palm Beach West" to distinguish it from West Palm Beach. The worst town on the list, number 38, was Haverhill. Why? Because, "Most people just know it as that voracious speed trap on Belvedere Road just west of Military Trail." As for Glen Ridge, (#30), "The entire town is only 100 acres." But the entire town is also a bird sanctuary. The population of Cloud Lake (#34), is only 139. What about Palm Beach itself? Why does it only rate seventh place? It's "Manicured paranoia. Basically, Disneyland without the rides." Of course, the number one spot goes to West Palm Beach itself. Random factoid: "Police once tried to stop drug dealing on a corner by installing speakers on a nearby building and blasting classical music. But somebody shot the speakers."

When I entered the C. H. Parsons shop, Marisol, the sales clerk, offered to assist me but seemed unable to find a jacket in my size on the racks, even though I showed her the size on the label of the jacket I was wearing, which I had bought from another store in their chain. Finally, she found a jacket that fit me, but it was the wrong color; I wanted blue, and all she could find was beige. I suggested checking the store's website. Alas, Marisol demonstrated her lack of computer skills and the company's disinterest in training its employees, since she was unable to accomplish this simple task.

There was only one other sales clerk in the store, an overweight, gruff and thoroughly unpleasant man who did not make even the slightest effort to assist his hapless colleague, even though there were no other customers in the shop. It appeared to me that he would have preferred his company to lose the sale rather than assist Marisol, whom he obviously detested.

While Marisol was fumbling with the computer, I walked around the store and came across a shelf of close-outs. This looked interesting! The first thing I found was a light blue, 100% cotton oxford cloth dress shirt (made in Indonesia). List price $89.95. Sale price: $24.98. Was it my size? Yes. Sold! I kept plowing through the stacks of close-outs, wondering what else I might find. Bingo! A pair of cotton twill Bermuda shorts (made in Sri Lanka). My size. Sale price: $3.98. Sold!

I took the items to the check-out desk to see if Marisol had been able to find my jacket. She hadn't.

It was noon on the dot and I was hungry, so I told her that I would pay for shirt and shorts, go have lunch and come back afterwards.

When I returned, Marisol had found the jacket, but couldn't figure out how to order it. As she continued to struggle with the computer, I resumed wandering around the store and discovered some silk ties on close-out. One of them (made in China) had a pattern of tiny seagulls perched on pilings over a light blue background: it could easily have been mistaken for one of those fancy French Hermès ties that retail for $195.00. Sale price: $7.98. Sold!

I took the tie back to the check-out desk. Marisol had finally located the jacket. It, too, was on sale: only $175.95. "I'll take it." But it had to be paid for in advance No problem. She asked for my personal data. I gave her my name and address, even spelling them, but Marisol appeared to be so unfamiliar with the English language that she couldn't even spell my name correctly.

At that point, I snapped. I had had enough of Marisol's incompetence and her colleague's passive aggression. "I can't handle this! I'll pay for the tie and go." Marisol didn't even put up much resistance or even offer much of an apology; she just mumbled something about "The Computer." *Right,* I thought, *always blame the computer.*

So, although I didn't find my jacket, I was still a satisfied customer. Total cost of my three purchases: $39.16. As I walked out of the store, I murmured a silent "thank you" to the anonymous seamstresses in Indonesia, Sri Lanka and China who had toiled in their sweatshops sewing the garments I had just purchased for a song.

Since I still hadn't found my blue sportscoat, the next day I went to City Place in West Palm Beach. Unlike The Mall at Wellington Green, it is open-air. It reminded me of a shopping plaza I had visited in San José, Costa Rica, many years ago: everything was outdoors. It's as if the promoters of City Place had wanted to create a Disneyland version of the main street of a small Midwestern town of yesteryear, one of the hundreds of hometowns in the heartland of America whose mom-and-pop stores were driven into bankruptcy by monopolistic conglomerates and are now boarded up and abandoned.

Rosemary Avenue is the main street of City Place. This outdoor mall is anchored on one end by a supermarket, and on the other end, by a pizzeria complementing its fare with dozens of craft ales on tap. Between the two is Schradsky's, a safari-themed retailer of clothing and accessories. I stopped in to see if I could find my sportscoat.

Although the label in the sportscoat the saleswoman showed me indicated that it was my size, it wasn't. It was cut too small. There were no larger sizes. As I prepared to leave the shop, she asked me if I needed anything else. As a matter of fact, I did: a sweatshirt. She accompanied me to a rack and helped me find a navy blue, hooded sweatshirt (made in China). The label showed that the original list price had been $89.50. It had first been marked down to $69.99 and then to $36.99. But since I was a new customer, I got an additional 20% discount, which brought the final price down to $29.59. Sold! Assuming that, even at $29.95, the garment was sold at a profit, the original price of $89.50 would have generated an astronomical mark-up for the company.

I still hadn't found my sportscoat, so I returned to the Mall at Wellington Green mall a few days later and decided to check out some of the other stores. I first went to Gimbels, a large department store, whose merchandise was displayed on two levels. After helping me purchase a bottle of men's fragrance, Anne-Marie escorted me to the Men's Department, where her colleague Paul promptly showed me a beautiful navy blue, tropical-weight Hart, Schaffner & Marx sportscoat. It fit like a glove. The label bore an American flag and proclaimed that it was "Made in USA." I was surprised to find apparel that was actually manufactured in the United States.

Determined to learn more about the textile industry in the United States, subsequently I conducted some research. According to an article by Philip Shenon entitled "Made in the U.S.A.? Hard Labor on a Pacific Island," published in the *New York Times* in 1993, thousands of garment workers, 90% of whom were young women, from China, the Philippines and elsewhere in Asia, were flown to the island of Saipan, the largest of an archipelago of fourteen islands in the Pacific known as the Commonwealth of the Northern Mariana Islands.

Shenon writes, "Often bused straight from the airport to squalid barracks where they lived as many as a dozen to a room, they were put to work almost immediately in nearby factories...many of them laboring six days a week at about half the Federal minimum, stitching together American brand-name clothes, whose labels would be familiar to anyone who has strolled through an American shopping mall..." At the industry's height, in the mid-to late 1900's, as many as 36 factories employed over 15,000 contract workers. Clothing made in the Northern Marianas often carried another familiar label: "Made in USA."

How was this possible? Simply because the Commonwealth of the Northern Mariana Islands is an overseas territory of the United States. Native-born residents of the commonwealth are American citizens and send their own delegate to the House of Representatives[21] along with Puerto Rico, the U.S. Virgin Islands, Guam, American Samoa and—lest we forget—the District of Columbia, whose license plates bear the inscription "Taxation without Representation" because the 600,000 American

---

[21] Since January 6, 2009, the Commonwealth has been represented in Congress by Gregorio Kilili Camacho Sablan.

citizens who live there pay Federal taxes but have no voting representation in either the House or Senate. These six delegates are allowed to introduce legislation and vote in committees but, like children, they are not considered grown-up enough to vote for passage of legislation in the full House. Furthermore, the citizens of these six territories are deprived of any representation whatsoever in the United States Senate, in clear violation of the intent of the Founding Fathers.

Mike Lofgren, a former senior analyst on the House and Senate Budget Committees, discussed the Saipan garment factories in his best-seller, *The Party is Over*.[22] Lofgren reports that "the territory was exempt from U.S. wage and workplace safety laws…there were persistent reports of near-gulag labor conditions, including barbed wire around the factories…Forced abortions were among the abuses reportedly taking place against female workers who became pregnant." The entrepreneurs hired lobbyist Jack Abramoff—later sentenced to six years in federal prison for mail fraud, conspiracy to bribe public officials and tax evasion—to lobby Capitol Hill. Abramoff's crony, the then Republican House Majority Leader Tom DeLay, ensured that the House never considered legislation to end the abuses. [23]

---

[22] *The Party Is Over: How the Republicans Went Crazy, Democrats Became Useless and the Middle Class Got Shafted*, New York, Viking, 2012.

[23] DeLay was convicted in 2011 of conspiracy to violate election law, but was acquitted in 2014 on appeal.

Currently, there are no garment factories operating on Saipan, and the sweatshop era has come to an end. Their demise was not due to action by Congress, but because quotas for textile exports to the United States expired in 2005. Production was shifted from Saipan to China, Vietnam, Bangladesh, Pakistan and Cambodia where the minimum wage was far below Saipan's "generous" $4.05 an hour. Almost twenty-six years after the first factory opened in October, 1983, the last one closed on January 15, 2009. [24]

Once upon a time, some of the most elegant and sought-after apparel in the world was manufactured in America. Back in 1895, Amos Sulka, a businessman born in Berlin, and Leon Wormser, a custom shirt-maker who had emigrated from Alsace, jointly opened a haberdashery on lower Broadway in New York. Starting with custom-made uniforms for firefighters and policemen, A. Sulka & Co. grew to cultivate a clientele of movie stars, royalty and statesmen. Sulka specialized in luxury garments for the carriage trade—high-quality shirts and silk ties, scarfs, smoking jackets, sleeping coats and dressing gowns—and exotic items such as vicuña sweaters, cashmere pullovers and alpaca vests. The firm bought a textile mill in Lyons,

---

[24] The most recent controversial activity on Saipan and the newest boon to the local economy is a phenomenon known as birth tourism, in which pregnant women from China fly to Saipan for delivery. According to the provisions of the Fourteenth Amendment, their children automatically become American citizens. More than one-third of the births in the Northern Marianas in 2012 were to Chinese birth tourists.

France, to supply their fabrics. In 1904, a Sulka store opened at 2, rue de Castiglione, on the corner of the Rue de Rivoli, perhaps the most prestigious address in Paris. After Amos Sulka died in 1946, the company opened branches in Chicago and San Francisco. Unable to adapt to changing fashions of the 1960's and 1970's, the firm was sold to a succession of owners before finally shutting its doors in 2001 and 2002. A "Sulka" mosaic can still be seen on the sidewalk outside the location of the Paris shop, a mute reminder to passersby of the firm's past glory.

What about that sportscoat? I was gratified to learn that Hart, Schaffner & Marx clothing is, indeed, "Made in USA." by well-paid American citizens, and not "Made on Saipan" by imported Asian wage-slaves. The firm's corporate headquarters are located in Chicago and the garments are manufactured in Des Plaines, Illinois, at a union shop. Hart, Schaffner & Marx started making suits in 1887 when Grover Cleveland was president, and President Barack Obama orders his suits from the company: his favorite is a two-button, wool-cashmere blend. An off-the-rack version of Obama's suit retailed for about $1,500 in 2008.

Alas, the price of the American-made Hart, Schaffner & Marx wool blazer was $459.00 plus 6% Florida sales tax. "Thank you, Paul."

Determined to find a sportscoat within my budget, I continued exploring the mall. As I was on my way to Gimbels, I stopped in my tracks: Steckler's was offering 40% discounts on the store's entire merchandise during the Memorial Day weekend. Steckler's is a high-end chain of menswear, so the prospect of a substantial discount was an enticement I could not ignore. Sally promptly helped me find my heart's desire, a tropical-weight, navy blue sportscoat in my size (made in China). List price: $299.50. Applying the discount brought the price down to $179.70, just 70 cents more than Marisol's jacket at Parson's. I was so elated with the successful outcome to my quest that I celebrated by treating myself a dress shirt, also at a 40% discount. It was made in Malaysia.

"Chickens aren't vegetarians!"

I.

Back in the 1970's, when Monique and I would go for day hikes in the countryside surrounding Paris, we always carried a hinged, plastic box with compartments for a half-dozen eggs. We would often stop at a farm where a hand-lettered sign announced *Œufs Frais* or even *Œufs du Jour*. We could see the hens roaming freely in the barnyard, clucking contentedly as they feasted on tasty bugs and worms and leftover peelings from the kitchen. We would always stop and chat with the *fermière* and leave with six freshly-laid eggs in our

117

backpack. The French believe that only fresh eggs should be served soft-boiled so, for the next day or two, we would start breakfast with those farm-fresh eggs, their yolks often colored almost orange. In the last decade, I have only found fresh farm eggs for sale twice during my hikes in the same areas around Paris.

II.

The interest in organic food has been growing exponentially in recent years, with chains of organic food stores proliferating and the mainstream chains are adding more and more organic foods to their shelves. Unfortunately, a lot of people have confused "organic" with "vegetarian." That's not the case.

Concomitant with the organic movement, millions of consumers have turned away from beef, whose sales have plummeted as poultry sales have skyrocketed. But there is beef and there is beef just as there is poultry and poultry. Herds of cattle in Argentina and France, and increasingly in the United States, graze free-range in the open air and munch on grass, producing the tenderest and tastiest beef. Their manure becomes part of the compost heap. On the other hand, cattle that are shipped to feedlots, fed a regimen of corn and injected with growth hormones become morbidly obese because, being ruminants, they are unable to properly digest cereal grains.

It's the same with poultry: approximately 90% of the egg-laying hens in the United States are crammed into battery cages inside gargantuan chicken factories lit with artificial lighting for long periods of time. The cages are so small and the birds so crowded together that they are unable stretch their wings or engage in natural behaviors such as dust-bathing and perching. They are fed a diet of cereal grains and additives instead of foraging in a natural environment outdoors. Unsurprisingly, like cattle, they, too, become morbidly ill: a battery hen's lifespan varies between one and three years; a backyard chicken may reach an age of five to seven years.

III.

Washington Post staff writer Peter Whoriskey published an article in its issue of April 29, 2015, entitled provocatively "People love chickens that are 'vegetarian fed.' But chickens are not vegetarians." For the first time, I saw written confirmation of what I had known since those days back in France: chickens, as all poultry, are omnivores, and do best on a vegetable and insectivorous diet. Whoriskey continues, "Forced vegetarianism can be a disaster" for chickens because the diet lacks an essential protein-based amino acid known as methionine. Without it, they fall ill. Not only that, "The birds will also turn on each other, pecking at each other...and these incidents can escalate into a hen house bloodbath." Consequently, most chickens raised commercially

119

in the United States are debeaked to prevent cannibalism, feather pecking and vent pecking. Whoriskey goes on to quote Blake Alexandre, whose 30,000 chickens pasture free-range in northern California: "They're really like little raptors—they want meat…The idea that they ought to be vegetarians is ridiculous."

Blake Alexandre's opinion is supported by Kathryn Bax in the article, "What do Chickens Eat?" on her Countryfarm Lifestyles website: "Chickens need a daily amount of protein in their diet…Giving meat scraps, meal worms and fish to your chickens is important, especially if your chickens don't have access to new grass every day. If they did, they would be getting their protein needs from grasshoppers, bugs and earthworms."

It gets worse. Because millions of chickens are confined in insalubrious egg factories, epidemics of H5N2 avian flu occur with alarming frequency. The Associated Press reported on May 6, 2015, that the bird flu virus was present in more than 100 farms in the Midwest with more than 28 million birds affected. An estimated 21 million chickens and half a million turkeys needed to be destroyed in 11 Iowa counties, and another 7 million birds in Wisconsin and Minnesota were expected to be destroyed as well. Iowa's Department of Natural Resources issued three temporary permits to a Massachusetts company to set up portable incinerators in three counties.

This inhumane hecatomb is the direct consequence of the massive, industrialized production of eggs and poultry.

IV.

One Sunday morning, I decided to go shopping at the celebrated Palm Beach Publix on The Island, considered the company's diadem. Although it offers valet parking to prevent the customers from backing their Bentleys into one another in the parking lot, I only saw a janitor sweeping outside the front door. Maybe the valets get Sundays off. There were no Bentleys in the parking lot either; perhaps the uber-rich sleep in on Sunday. I roamed the spacious aisles, first stopping to spend some time in the wine section. As I expected, the store had a wide variety, arranged according to country of origin. Another section was devoted exclusively to organic and biodynamic wines—American, Chilean, Argentine, Italian and South African—but, surprisingly, none from France. Since there were so few customers, I was able to have a long conversation with Nestor, the cheese manager.

I reasoned that if any store would have "real" eggs, it would be this one. There was quite a variety on the shelves, including boxes of pasteurized eggs, "gently heated in a bath of warm water" and the expected "grain-fed" eggs. I passed them up when I saw something called "4 Grain All Natural" eggs. The label reassured apprehensive vegetarians that "no animal fat or animal byproducts" were added to the chickenfeed, which consisted of grains and "protein-rich soybean meal." They cost half as much as the organic eggs, so I decided to try a dozen on the pretext that, although the hens were not supplementing their regimen with delicious bugs and worms and nibbling on tasty leftover veggies or "animal by-products," at least they were getting some protein in their diet. I cooked a couple the next morning; although the label invited consumers to "taste the difference," the only difference I could detect between these and the vegetarian eggs was the color of the shells: these were white, the vegetarian ones were brown. As my grandmother would have said, I got stung.

I noticed on the label that these "4 Grain All Natural" eggs were produced by Cal-Maine Foods, Inc. and concluded that their hens must have been confined in those industrial-sized henhouses, too, and I regretted my purchase even more. When I checked the Cal-Maine website and saw an aerial view of one of the firm's gargantuan egg factories I was even more disheartened to discover that the company was "the largest producer and distributor of fresh shell eggs in the United States."

The company also markets "Cage-Free" eggs but, alas, the hens are still fed "a feed comprised of four high-quality grains, corn, flax, milo and wheat. What is "milo," anyway? I looked it up: according to the Wikipedia, it's a common name for some varieties of commercial sorghum. It's also used as fodder for cattle. Great.

V.

A writer friend in northern California has raised chickens all her life and possesses an encyclopedic knowledge of animal husbandry. After I wrote her about the French eggs with those orange yolks, she responded:

> As an old and adventurous chicken farmer, I have to say that the color of the yolk is greatly influenced by the breed of chicken. My Buff Orpingtons, a big wonderfully fluffy-rumped very friendly bird, have a much lighter colored yolk than, say, the common Rhode Island Red. And then too...the yolk color is influenced by what they eat. My Buffs ate quite a few pests from the orchard, including bright green grasshoppers, which gave their yokes a bit of a greenish tinge...They used to follow me around, clucking peaceably.

Green yolks or not, those were real eggs. Perhaps my friend's green eggs inspired Dr. Seuss, whose popular children's book, *Green Eggs and Ham*, concludes with Sam-I-Am's unnamed interlocutor observing, "I do so like green eggs and ham. Thank you. Thank you, Sam-I-Am."

VI.

It would seem that the only way to obtain "real" eggs today is either raise your own chickens or buy them from a farmer like Blake Alexandre, who allows his chickens to roam in their pasture and savor that delicious, naturally-occurring diet. A friend in France wrote me that some towns in that country now donate pairs of layers to qualified households, whose members are required to feed them their biodegradable vegetable and animal leftovers that otherwise would be tossed into the garbage can. Each hen consumes an average of 100 kilos [220 lbs.] of table scraps per year.

There's good news from America, too. A high-school classmate of mine who lives in Tennessee wrote me that chickens are the "in thing" in that part of the country. They are the only animal allowed to be raised within the city limits of Knoxville, and a lot of "big, fancy houses" have chickens running around in the front yard and coops in the back. And my friend in California, a transplanted Downeaster from Maine, reported that "Every town in Maine now has an ordinance allowing back-yard chickens and beehives. It's a whole big deal. Roosters are crowing at dawn in toney Cape Elizabeth!"

More good news appeared in the *Washington Post* of August 7, 2016. Karen Brulliard reported that in the past two years nearly 200 U.S. companies, including every major grocery and fast-food chain, that together buy half of the 7 billion eggs laid monthly, had pledged to use only cage-free eggs by 2025. That is certainly progress, but an uncaged, free-range bird only enjoys between 2.0 and 21.8 sq. ft. of space, whereas a pasture-raised bird can roam over an area of over 100 sq. ft. and forage freely on a diet of plants and obtain protein from insects and worms.

VII.

I abandoned my quest for eggs laid by omnivorous chickens until I paid a visit to the West Palm Beach Green Market. Located on the Waterfront Commons, it has been open every Saturday since 1994 from nine o'clock in the morning to one o'clock in the afternoon from October through May. The market was included in *Cooking Light* magazine's list of America's Best 50 Farmers' Markets, which includes one market per state. Over 70 vendors, most of whose small family farms are located in Palm Beach County, offer consumers fresh, locally grown fruits, vegetables, plants and other agricultural products ranging from organic meats to imported French cheeses. There's honey, too: saw palmetto, seagrape, sourwood and gallberry—and the rare tupelo honey, made famous in the film *Ulee's Gold*, produced in the Apalachicola and Ochlockonee River basins in the Florida Panhandle, predominantly in and near the town of Wewahitchka. You can even find Florida truffles in the Green Market.

As soon as I entered the market I spotted the stand of Ms. V's Organics. Veronica Niebur is Ms. V's real name, and her farm is located at nearby Lantana. Her associate Dani—short for Danielle—was staffing the stand, dispensing organic produce and honey from hives on the farm along with cartons of fresh eggs with shells of various shades and sizes, laid by hens of several different breeds. I learned that this flock was supervised by a rooster named Dexter who enjoyed riding around the farm and overseeing his domain from his perch on the hood of a golf cart.

Dani told me that she had spent time in Guyana, where chickens are mainly fed a diet of rice. The yolks were so pale that the cooks in the hotel where she was staying added yellow food coloring to them to give the illusion that they were real eggs. Unfortunately, the practice of feeding chickens rice has spread to Japan, where eggs with pale yolks are considered a luxury and fetch premium prices! When I inquired about the diet of Ms. V's chickens, I was pleasantly surprised to learn that they spent all day outdoors feasting on "all kinds of bugs" and that Ms. V only fed them grain to lure them into the henhouse at night so they could roost safe from predators.

VIII.

Back in the 1950's, when my family would visit my paternal grandmother, Laura Jane Kenyon, who lived in the small town of Oxford, in rural Benton County, Indiana, she always had a flock of chickens. Over the years, she accumulated, piece by piece, a service for eight of Haviland Limoges dinnerware. She paid for all of it with her egg money.

"Let's Get Married!"

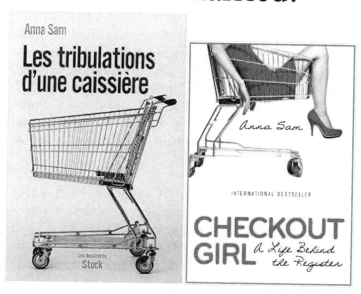

I.

Walmart is the world's largest publicly-traded retail distribution company with more than 2,000,000 employees and 8,500 stores in 15 countries worldwide—including over 4,000 in the United States alone. Although Walmart is nominally a publicly-traded company, control rests firmly in the hands of the six living heirs of founder Sam Walton, who own a majority of the shares. This Gang of Six possessed a combined net worth estimated at $144,700,000,000.00 in 2016—that's billions, not millions—making it the richest family in the United States, if not the world.

Like all little boys, former Walmart CEO Samuel Robson "Rob" Walton (net worth $32.4 billion, give or take a few billion) likes playing with cars, except that his toys are vintage Ferraris costing millions of dollars: in 2009 he bought a 1957 Ferrari 250 Testa Rossa for $12.1 million, a world record at the time. A few years later, another was sold for $39.8 million, so Rob could probably argue that he got a bargain.

Meanwhile, according to a company fact sheet dated January 20, 2016, entry-level Walmart wage-slaves, euphemistically known as "associates," are paid starvation wages of $9 an hour and will eventually reach a rate of $13.38 per hour. That is still lower than the average hourly rate for U.S. retail workers, which is $14.95, according to the Labor Department. Furthermore, instead of hiring full-time employees, in 2013 Walmart shifted its hiring policies to increase the number of temporary employees, who enjoy even fewer rights and benefits than full-time workers.

Unsurprisingly, approximately 70% of Walmart's workers quit within the first year. Not one of Walmart's 1.4 million American employees belongs to a union. The company is so ferociously opposed to unions that, when the "associates" of a Walmart in Jonquière, Québec, expressed their legal right to form a union in 2005, the Walmart bosses promptly retaliated by closing the store and throwing 190 employees into the street.

Walmart pay is so low that new hires are encouraged to apply for U.S. Government financial assistance under the Supplemental Nutrition Assistance Program (SNAP), known colloquially as "food stamps." According to Jobs for Justice, the scam consists of three phases: (1) paying employees so little that they are forced to rely on food stamps to survive. (2) Exploiting loopholes to avoid paying billions in taxes that fund food stamps. (3) Reaping billions in profits when food stamps are spent in Walmart stores. Thus Walmart extorts money from millions of American taxpayers to subsidize its employees because the Walton heirs are too greedy to pay them a living wage. Citing a report prepared by Americans for Tax Justice, *Forbes* reported on April 15, 2014, that Walmart workers cost taxpayers $6.2 billion annually in public assistance.

II.

Ten years or so ago, a French supermarket cashier named Anna Sam started a blog called *Caissière no future* and expanded it into a book entitled *Les tribulations d'une caissière,* published in 2008. Anna Sam's "tribulations" were amply rewarded because the book was translated into 21 languages, sold half a million copies worldwide and was adapted for the screen by Pierre Rambaldi. Anna Sam collected a colossal amount of money in royalties and penned a sequel that appeared the following year. I had a copy of her first book and after reading it offered it to one of the cashiers at my local Carrefour supermarket whom I had befriended, asking her to share with her colleagues.

III.

The difference between Walmart and Publix is that when you walk in the door, all the Walmart employees—if you can find any—look like they're at a funeral, whereas all the Publix employees look like they're having a party. It's glum *versus* happy, dejected *versus* upbeat.

I am on a first-name basis with all the cashiers at the Publix store in my neighborhood: Amber and Bertha and Beverly and Cathy-with-a-C and Kathy-with-a-K and Dawn and Edna and Vanessa...Most speak fluent Spanish as well as unaccented English, so I chat and flirt with them in both languages at check-out. Flirting is socially acceptable in Spanish, as it is in French. Spanish even possesses a lexicon of expressions known as *piropos* that men—and women—employ when flirting. The one *piropo* I always remember and use when the occasion permits is typical: *Por donde caminas, nacen flores.* "Wherever you walk, flowers bloom." I tried it out on my Colombian dental hygienist: she laughed and told me I was "cute." What better thing in the world could a man wish for than to make a lady laugh? There's even a website proposing an anthology of a thousand *piropos románticos y profundos* that can be memorized by suitors who aren't poetic.

Recently I had been discussing racism with a South African of my acquaintance as we entered the Publix. He contended that, from his personal experience, racial discrimination still existed in hiring practices. I maintained that things were improving and that young people today are less racist, on the whole, than their parents, far less racist than their grandparents, and less homophobic, too, due in large part to the visibility of prominent gays, lesbians and African-Americans in sports and entertainment, not to mention the highest elective office in the land.

As we walked in the door and my interlocutor headed for the vegetable bins, I was waylaid by Amber, one of the cashiers. "How are you today, honey?" she called out cheerily.

"We've been solving the problems of the world. I maintain that young people today are less racist than their parents."

"That is exactly what the author of a book was saying on C-SPAN the other day."

I stopped in my tracks. "C-SPAN? Were you watching C-SPAN?"

"Sure. I watch it all the time. I can't remember the author's name, but I'll find it for you."

I was so astonished to learn that Amber had been watching interviews with authors on C-SPAN that I exclaimed, "You are the first woman I have ever met who watches C-SPAN." The general consensus is that C-SPAN is the most boring channel on the airwaves. It doesn't even have any of those informative and entertaining commercials from drug companies pushing outrageously priced pills and nostrums and encouraging viewers to "ask your doctor" about maladies that didn't even exist five years ago.

"I watch it all the time. I'm a C-SPAN addict."

I couldn't resist boldly asking her an impolite question. "Are your married?"

"No, I'm not."

"Let's get married," I blurted. "We can watch C-SPAN together. We can sit on the couch drinking chilled chardonnay and argue about which C-SPAN channel we should watch." By that time, customers were lining up for check-out and becoming more and more impatient, so I hastily took my leave of Amber and set out to do my shopping.

IV.

I ordered a copy of *Checkout Girl: A Life Behind the Register*, the English adaptation of Anna Sam's book, and offered it to Amber, just as I had offered the original to her French sister.

Readers of this book are invited to the wedding.

Highwaymen

Back in the 1950's when my family was taking those annual vacations to Florida, we might have noticed a painting in one of the low-budget motels without air conditioning where we sweltered in those sultry summers. It would have been a quintessential representation of a mythical Florida borne in the mind of every tourist to Florida then and still carried by some today despite the high-rises, the interstate highways and Disneyworld: swaying palm trees, pristine sandy beaches, the surf, sunrises over the Atlantic, Royal Poinciana trees drenched in scarlet flowers and maybe a blue heron or a snowy egret spearing fish in a tranquil river. We wouldn't have known or cared who painted them, and we certainly wouldn't have recognized the artist's name if we saw it, since for most of their careers they worked in obscurity.

Approximately 200,000 of those paintings were executed from the mid-1950's through the mid-1980's by a group of 26 self-taught and self-mentoring African-American artists, 25 men and one woman, from in and around Fort Pierce, on the Atlantic Coast. Back in those days, most jobs for African-American men in Florida were either picking fruit in the orange groves, cutting sugar cane or working in the slaughterhouses and meat packers for $15 a day; women spent their time keeping house and tending to the children. Yet

133

some had an artistic bent and a fortunate few, including Alfred Hair and Harold Newton, whose art now sells for the highest prices, were influenced by and received encouragement from a prominent white painter named A. E. Backus, who specialized in vivid Floridian landscapes. These artists are now known as the Florida Highwaymen or, simply, the Highwaymen, a term coined by Jim Fitch, a gallery owner and early collector of their art, because they would often shuttle up and down U.S. Route 1 along the coast between Miami and Jacksonville, sometimes selling their paintings to tourists from the trunks of their cars parked along the side of the road.

A number of the future Highwaymen studied art at Lincoln Park Academy[25] in Fort Pierce with Zenobia Jefferson. The academy was founded in 1906 to provide quality education to African-American students. Today, it is a nationally-recognized magnet school with high entrance requirements. Since in the segregated South of the 1950's and 1960's, no galleries would display their work, the young artists sold to doctors, lawyers and businessmen to display in their offices and to restaurants and motels to enhance the décor of their dining rooms. They asked between $10 and $45 for their paintings; today, works by the lesser-known artists can be acquired by collectors for hundreds of

---

[25] Ralph P. Stregles, discussed elsewhere in this book, taught at Lincoln Park Academy in 1987-89.

dollars and older pieces by the most renowned members of the group fetch many thousands.

I know that we must have driven past those cars as we sped along U.S. Route 1, but I doubt that my father, a mechanical engineer who did not care for art and was frugal to a fault, would ever have considered stopping to squander his money on one of these pictures.

A number of the original Highwaymen, most born in the 1930's, are deceased. Among them, Alfred Hair died in 1970 and Harold Newton in 1994. However, most of their friends and colleagues, including Highwaywoman Mary Ann Carroll, have continued painting Florida in their same idealized style.

Certainly the most prolific all the Highwaymen is James Gibson, who studied with Zenobia Jefferson and whose gifts were also recognized by Backus. "He told me that talent was talent no matter what color the artist," Gibson recalled in an interview. "It was probably the nicest thing anyone had ever said to me."

According to the biography posted on his personal website, James Gibson was born on January 1, 1938, and is a fourth-generation Floridian. I had the good fortune to meet Mr. Gibson on February 29, 2016, the day he delivered closing remarks at an exposition of Highwayman art at the Grassy Waters Preserve in West Palm Beach. He is not only a prolific artist, but a gifted raconteur who regaled the standing-room-only crowd with many Real Stories from his long career.

In one of Mr. Gibson's anecdotes, he recalled that sometime in the early 1960's he was pulled over by a Florida state trooper when he was at the wheel of his brand new Chevrolet Impala. "Whose car is this?" the suspicious trooper demanded imperiously. Gibson, who was brought up to always be impeccably dressed, drew himself up tall and replied, "I am an artist and I have some of my paintings in the trunk. Would you like to see them?" The trooper was so impressed that he bought two on the spot. Mr. Gibson remarked that although he usually sold them for $35 apiece, he offered the trooper a bargain price of two for $45. But the story didn't end there. As Gibson continued down the highway, the trooper pulled up again: he had spoken to a Palm Beach police captain who needed some art to adorn the walls of the new station. "The captain asked when I could come down to the station with my paintings. I said, I'll come right now. In fifteen minutes I sold all the paintings I had in the trunk of my Chevy to off-duty police officers, FBI agents and troopers."

We also learned how Mr. Gibson befriended then-governor Jeb Bush. Traveling to Tallahassee, he visited the capitol building hoping to sell some of his paintings to decorate the governor's office. The official was encouraging, and asked Gibson to bring some of them with him the next he came to town. Mr. Gibson, who never left home without his paintings, replied that he had some in the trunk of his car. Governor Bush happened to be in his office that day, and he liked Gibson's work so much that he acquired a painting of a Royal Poinciana that now graces the governor's office. "There's no such thing as an ugly Poinciana," observed Mr. Gibson.

Governor Bush subsequently commissioned Mr. Gibson to produce four more pieces, and works by him and by other Highwaymen hang in the Florida state capitol building where they have been commissioned by three other sitting governors.

"I'm a big fan of his work," Bush declared in a profile of Gibson that appeared in *People* in its issue of August 11, 2003, "He can capture Florida in just a few brush strokes, and his history makes his work even more amazing." According to an article in the *Palm Beach Post* dated February 15, 2015, works by the Highwaymen also hang in the White House, where they were purchased by Presidents Lyndon Johnson and George W. Bush, as well as by Vice President Hubert Humphrey.

Whereas in the old days, James Gibson and the other Highwaymen traveled along U.S. Route 1 looking for customers, nowadays he occasionally hits the highway again, not to sell his new paintings, but to seek out old ones at garage sales and antique shops. Once, in 2002, he spotted an authentic James Gibson in an antique shop in Saint Augustine,: the price tag was $1,000.00.

After his lecture, I had the opportunity to speak with Mr. Gibson. He had explained that he continues to maintain the Highwayman tradition of speed painting by working simultaneously on several canvasses, lining them up and applying one layer of pigment at a time, first the backgrounds, then the foregrounds, then the shadows. This piqued my curiosity and I asked him to estimate how many works he had painted in all these years. With a mischievous smile, he replied, "I stopped counting at ten thousand."

"I don't need twenty dollars."

I.

Since 1998, tourists and residents of West Palm can travel free of charge on four trolley lines shuttling to and from museums, the Palm Beach Outlets mall, the Tri-Rail train station, the Kravis Center for the Performing Arts, the restaurants, shops and cinema in City Place and the Mandel Public Library. The eleven vehicles in the city-owned fleet are not trolleys in the classic sense, since they aren't powered by electricity obtained from an overhead cable and they don't run on rails; instead, they are small buses built on truck chassis and powered by internal-combustion engines running on LPG—liquid propane gas. According to the website of the manufacturer, Double K, Inc., in Crandon, Wisconsin, the vehicles are designed "in replica of the nostalgic streetcars of the early 1800's."

One day, I had done some shopping and was sitting on the bench at the bus stop waiting for the trolley to take me home. There was a man in his 50s sitting on the bench, too, and we struck up a conversation. His name was Fred, and this is his Real Story.

"Around noon yesterday I was sitting on this bench making a bologna and cheese sandwich when a woman stopped by and asked me what I was doing.

I replied that I was fixing my lunch. She asked me what I was making and I told her it was a bologna and cheese sandwich, but that I really would like to have a hot chicken sandwich because I had been eating bologna and cheese sandwiches for the past three weeks."

Fred explained to me that he was homeless and continued his narrative.

"When she heard that, she took a $20 bill out of her purse and offered it to me. 'I don't need twenty dollars,' I replied, 'I just need $4.89 to buy a hot chicken sandwich.'

"The lady adamantly insisted that I take the money. Again, I refused. 'I don't need twenty dollars. I just need $4.89.'

"The lady was in a quandary. Finally, she declared, 'I'm going to give you this $20 bill and I want you to take it. You go into that store and buy yourself your hot chicken sandwich. I'll be coming back tomorrow morning and you can give me the change at that time.'"

"Did you ever see her again?"

"This morning, around 8:30, she came back with her little granddaughter. She asked me if I had enjoyed my hot chicken sandwich. I replied that I had and that I had her change in my pocket. I took out fifteen dollars, eleven cents, and was prepared to hand it to her when she told me, 'Keep the rest of the money. You may want to buy another hot chicken sandwich in the future and you can use this money to pay for it.' With that, she went on her way."

I told Fred that that was a very interesting story and a very complex interpersonal relationship adding, "That lady had to trick you into taking that money without your losing your self-respect, didn't she?"

II.

About a week later I met Fred again. I had done some shopping and was sitting on the bench at the bus stop waiting for the trolley to take me home when Fred appeared looking much happier than when I had seen him previously. "I haven't seen you for a while," he told me, "I had been looking for you."

"Have you got another interesting encounter to tell me about?"

"You won't believe what happened a few days ago. I was sitting on this bench, where I usually sit, and a well-dressed, elderly man came up to me and asked me if my name was Fred. 'Yes, it is.' 'Have you had three heart attacks and did you lose your son when he was seven?' 'Yes, that's all true.' 'Can you show me your ID?' 'Sure, here it is.' I took out my driver's license and handed it to him."

Before continuing the story of his encounter with the mysterious stranger, Fred filled in some of the details of his past. Born and raised in a northern city, he had led a normal, middle-class life until his son was killed in the crossfire of a gang shootout while sitting on the steps in front of his house. Because of his loss, Fred turned to crack cocaine and his addiction ultimately led to his downfall. Fred took out his wallet and removed a glass tube about four inches long, with burn marks staining the bottom, which was closed. "This is a crack pipe. I've been clean for seven years but I keep it as I reminder of what I was. I could be arrested if this was found on me, but I explained to one of the local policemen the reason I was carrying it, so they don't bother me."

"But you are still running a risk carrying it, aren't you?"

He paused. "I suppose I am."

"I think you need to carry this risk with you. It's a symbol of the way you are living now, on the edge."

Fred put the pipe away. I later discovered (in an article in the business magazine *Forbes* of all places) that these glass tubes are made in China and come with a colored silk rose inside and a cork on the open end to keep the rose from falling out. They are purchased in bulk and sold as Love Roses or Roses in a Glass in convenience stores and gas stations for 99 cents apiece. The crack addicts buy them, then throw the silk roses away. Those who are so inclined can even buy a pretty box of 36 Love Roses of assorted colors on Amazon.com for just $8.90.

"I am still intrigued as to how this man was able to locate you here on this bench. And how did he know all those details about you?"

"I asked him the same questions. He told me, 'Don't waste your time trying to figure that out. God told me to find you and take care of you.' Then, he continued, 'My wife is on her way over here. How would you like a steak dinner? We'd like to invite you to the steakhouse up on the corner of Sapodilla and Okeechobee.' 'That place is too fancy for me. Look at the way I'm dressed; they'd never let me in.' I was in the same clothes I have on now."

In fact, Fred was dressed in the same sweat-stained olive green tee-shirt and scruffy denims he was wearing when I had seen him the previous week.

"The man replied, 'They'll let you in because you'll be with me.' And that's exactly what happened."

Fred continued, "That's not all. While we were waiting for the man's wife to arrive, he told me that he had found an apartment for me to live in over on Datura Avenue. 'I'll pay the rent each month and have the utilities bills sent to me. You won't pay a cent.'"

"So what happened next?"

"He told me that he had to leave town to take care of some business, but that he'd be back in three days to move me into the apartment."

I told Fred that his story reminded me of a weekly television series that ran from 1955 to 1960 called *The Millionaire*; in each episode the "fabulously wealthy" John Beresford Tipton Jr., who never appears on screen, donates a cashier's check for a million dollars to an ordinary citizen—some rich and some poor—and the viewers learn how the benefactor's million dollars change the life of the beneficiary—for better or worse. Fred was old enough that he remembered seeing it, too.

III.

I must believe that Fred's anonymous benefactor was a man of his word because, although I continued to sit on the bench at the bus stop waiting for the trolley to take me home, I never saw Fred again.

The Belle Glade Six

I. El Chapo

"On 11 July 2015, Joaquín Archivaldo Guzmán Loera escaped from Federal Social Readaptation Center No. 1, a maximum-security prison in Almoloya de Juárez, Mexico. After receiving medication, Guzmán, nicknamed "El Chapo," Spanish for "Shorty," because of his height, was last seen by security cameras at 20:52 hours near the shower area in his cell. The shower area was the only part of his cell that was not visible through the security camera. After the guards did not see him for twenty-five minutes on surveillance video, personnel went looking for him.

When they reached his cell, Guzmán was gone. It was discovered he had escaped through a tunnel leading from the shower area to a house construction site 1.5 km (0.93 miles) away in a Santa Juanita neighborhood. The tunnel lay 10 m (32.8 feet) deep underground, and Guzmán used a ladder to climb to the bottom. The tunnel was 1.7 m (5.7 feet) tall and 75 cm (29.5 inches) in width. It was equipped with artificial light, air ducts, and high-quality construction materials. In addition, a motorcycle was found in the tunnel, which authorities think was used to transport materials and possibly Guzmán himself. Although guards discovered that Guzmán had escaped at 21:22 hours, a "red alert," which locks down the prison and alerts a nearby military garrison, was only activated at midnight." [Source: Wikipedia]

II. Crime

El Chapo was not the first prisoner to gain his freedom through a tunnel. He might have learned his technique and drawn his inspiration from a sextet of Floridians who, on January 2, 1995, taking advantage of that fact that, because of the New Year's holiday, many corrections officers were taking the day off, escaped from the Glades Correctional Institution in Belle Glade, Florida, about 40 miles west of West Palm Beach.

All six escapees were serving minimum mandatory sentences of 25 years to life in the 1,200-bed state prison, most of whose inmates were also violent felons serving life sentences. This is their Real Story.

According to the South Florida *Sun-Sentinel*, Florencio Álvarez, 39; Armando R. Junco, 62; Hector Manuel Rivas, 32, Jesús Martinez, 47, Felix Carbonell, 34, and Juan Jesús Fleitas, 30, all of whom were born in Cuba and grew up in Miami, were some of the most cold-blooded killers ever apprehended in southern Florida. "Two of them blasted their victims with machine guns. Another shot his roommate in the head nine times and set him ablaze after an argument over a bag of pot. One threw a boat captain overboard and watched him drown. The fifth shot a restaurant patron dead during a robbery."

Described bizarrely in the *Miami New Times* as "a short thug cut like a chiseled underwear model," Fleitas had arrived during the 1980 Mariel boatlift and immediately began breaking into houses. The boatlift allowed 125,000 Cubans to leave the island and resettle in the United States; unfortunately, the Castro regime cynically utilized the exodus to empty Cuban prisons of all the most violent and hardened criminals and free many patients from mental health facilities. Consequently, more than 1,700 *Marielitos* were jailed or institutionalized in the United States.

Fleitas and an accomplice attempted to burglarize a house in West Hialeah, but when 21-year old Miguel Rudelando Pérez came home unexpectedly, Fleitas panicked and shot him three times in the face with a 45-caliber machine gun.

Florencio Álvarez used a MAC-10 submachine gun to kill his sleeping roommate, Evelio Valdez, after the two had argued about ownership of a bag of marijuana. Hector Manuel Rivas had murdered Key West charter-boat captain Hans Baumgartner, in an attempt to return to Cuba. Jesús Reyes Martinez had become angry and killed a patron who tried to chase him after a restaurant holdup. Like Fleitas, Armando Junco was a *Marielito* and was convicted in 1983 in Dade County after shooting two rival drug dealers and a farmer who heard the shots. Felix Carbonell had also murdered a man during a home invasion.

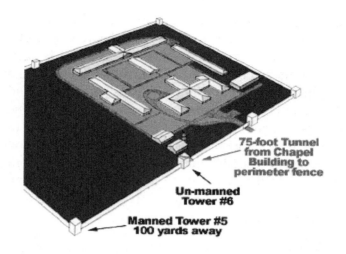

75-foot Tunnel
from Chapel
Building to
perimeter fence

Un-manned
Tower #6

Manned Tower #5
100 yards away

III. Escape and Capture

During their free time, the Belle Glade Six began
attending regular church services at the chapel
located only 40 feet from the prison's fence. But as
the *Washington Post* put it, "They were not singing
in the choir or rehearsing for the Christmas play.
They were digging." Built in 1947, the chapel was
later raised on stilts like many buildings in the area
to prevent it from sinking into the muck. The crawl
space underneath the chapel provided the perfect
cover for the inmates to excavate their tunnel.

According to the *Washington Post*, "Their escape
was straightforward but highly risky. The men had
pried loose a grate that allowed them to access the
crawl space. Once under the chapel, the men
apparently worked in shifts over a period of three

weeks, changing into spare uniforms for the dirty work of digging their tunnel and buttressing it with lumber stolen from a prison construction site." The Associated Press reported the tunnel was three feet under the surface and extended between 45 and 75 feet from the chapel to a point outside the prison fence. It was reported in the *Miami Herald* that the prisoners had used shovels and flashlights, one of which was said to have been purchased for $20 from a prison guard.

Prison authorities concluded that Fleitas had masterminded the escape and that he and four others had beaten up fellow inmate Felix Carbonell at the tunnel's exit, leaving him as bait for the guards and bloodhounds. Like El Chapo, Fleitas was operating a lucrative drug trade from inside the prison and, like El Chapo, is likely to have utilized some of his profits to buy protection and assistance on the outside, once he had escaped.

Carbonell, the fall guy, hid in a row of bushes, where he was captured immediately. According to the Florida Department of Corrections, a tip from two citizens to a Florida Highway Patrol station led to a dragnet resulting in the recapture of Álvarez and the death of Junco, who was killed by a Miami police officer during a shootout between the fugitives and the combined forces that included the Florida Department of Law Enforcement, the FBI and Miami and Metro-Dade police and resembled a scene out of *Bonnie and Clyde*. According to the *Sun-Sentinel*, Álvarez told police that he and Junco ended up in a squalid camp of homeless Cuban exiles after "a wild ride down U.S. 27 on top of a bucking semitrailer barreling away from the state prison." While they were in the camp, the two lived in a dirt-floor shack made of scrap wood and corrugated steel and befriended Manuel Vega, a fellow Cuban exile. Vega told authorities that he and the fugitives spent time discussing a common dream: going back to their native Cuba to topple the Castro regime, doubtlessly inspired by Cuban patriot José Martí's incursion against the Spanish occupiers of Cuba in the 1890's, which was prepared in Florida. Vega also stated that the two escaped convicts "had plenty of cash."

Rivas was caught next, 10 days after the escape, by a patrol officer who spotted him walking in the Little Havana *barrio* of Miami. Martinez was caught the next day, also in Little Havana, when he made the mistake of walking in front of a patrol car and was recognized. Fleitas would remain at large for the next two years.

IV. Punishment

Carbonell pleaded guilty to a charge of escape on August 19, 1995, and received a three-year sentence, ordered to run consecutively with his current sentence. Rivas was tried on September 16, 1996, on the same charge. At his trial, he admitted fleeing and was sentenced to an additional 15 years. On August 15, 1995, Martinez also pleaded guilty to attempted escape and, like Carbonell, received an additional three-year sentence. At his trial, he admitted fleeing the penitentiary and was also sentenced to an additional 15 years. Álvarez pleaded guilty on August 15, 1995, and was sentenced on September 1, 1995.

V. The Long Arm of the Law

or

Justice is Served

According to an article by Frances Robles and Manny García in the *Miami Herald* dated August 26, 1997, Juan Jesús Fleitas "remained on the lam until August 3, 1997, when Mexican police allege that he shot Dania Leva Fleitas[26] during a bungled robbery in Mérida, on the Yucatán Peninsula of Mexico." Like Ralph Stregles, discussed elsewhere in this book, Fleitas was an imposter, operating under one of his false identities, "Roberto García López," and working as a waiter and busboy at a seafood restaurant in a Mérida mall. Subsequent to the shooting, his picture appeared in a local newspaper and a tipster thought he bore a striking resemblance to Fleitas, who had been featured on *America's Most Wanted*. The tipster called the FBI, fingerprints were exchanged and they matched.

The U.S. law enforcement authorities requested Mexico to extradite Fleitas, but the procedure was delayed because he was now accused of attempted murder and a federal weapons-possession charge in

---

[26] The two are not related.

151

Mexico. In early November 1997, he was sentenced to nine years in prison on charges related to the attack in Mérida. Using his new persona of Roberto García López, Fleitas insisted he wasn't the fugitive from Belle Glade, repeatedly claiming mistaken identity. It was not until July 2011 that Juan Jesús Fleitas was finally extradited to Miami.

Barbara Piñeiro, head of Miami-Dade County's extradition unit, stated, "We really worked that case for fourteen straight years. It was almost constant pressures form our office to see that through." Fleitas was incarcerated again, in Florida, on July 29, 2011. Glades Correctional Institution was closed the same year and its inmates transferred elsewhere

The First Two Jewish Senators

The first two Jewish members of the United States Senate lived in Florida. One spent most of his life in the state, but the other only remained for a month since he was on the run from the Federal government and was traveling incognito to avoid capture. Both were born in the Virgin Islands. One died in New York and was buried in Washington. The other died and was buried in Paris. Each led extraordinary lives in and out of politics, yet both remain virtually forgotten today, perhaps because both supported the South in the Civil War.

David Levy Yulee (1810-1886)

David Levy was born of Sephardic parents on June 12, 1810, in Charlotte Amalie on the island of Saint Thomas, in the Danish West Indies, then under British occupation.[27] David's father, Moses Elias Levy, was born in 1781 in Essaouira (then known as Mogador), Morocco, the son of Eliahu Ha-Levi Ibn Yuli, an influential advisor to Sultan Mohammed ben Abdallah, an enlightened and tolerant monarch who invited Jews to settle and trade in Essaouira. Under Mohammed's reign, Morocco became the first nation to recognize the United States, in 1777.

---

[27] The Danish West Indies were acquired by the United States in 1917 for $25,000,000 in gold coin and renamed the United States Virgin Islands.

Following the sultan's death in 1790, Morocco experienced an outbreak of anti-Semitic atrocities and the Levy family crossed the 7-mile wide strait separating Africa from Europe and arrived on Gibraltar, where there were not only three synagogues, but a Jewish Masonic lodge, which Moses Levy joined. After the death of his father in 1800, Moses, his mother and his sister set sail for the Danish West Indies to join the community of Sephardim already living there. Moses became partners in a lumber business with Philip Benjamin, the father of Judah P. Benjamin, who would become the second Jewish United States Senator. After amassing a fortune in lumber, munitions and shipping in Cuba and Puerto Rico, he began to view his financial success as a moral burden, according to his biographer, historian Chris Monaco: "He feared that he was in danger of becoming what he most despised: a 'mere money-making animal.'"[28]

While in Cuba, Moses Elias Levy was attracted to Florida, still a Spanish possession, and purchased 100,000 acres of land in present-day Alachua County from Don Fernando de la Maza Arredondo with the intention of establishing Pilgrimage Plantation, a utopian Jewish colony, outside the town of Micanopy. Levy believed that Florida could be a new Zion, a home for the persecuted Jews of Europe. Jews in the Diaspora needed a homeland, a New Jerusalem, he observed, because "no

---

[28] Monaco, Chris, *Moses Levy of Florida: Jewish Utopian and Antebellum Reformer*, Baton Rouge: Louisiana State University Press, 2005.

amelioration can be expected at the hands of nations for us." Chris Monaco wrote that, "Levy believed the United States, like Noah's Mount Ararat, would serve as the final destination of his oppressed brethren and that a new era of agrarian prosperity would emerge to fulfill God's plan." The community was founded in 1821, and Levy invested in a state-of-the-art sugar mill, a blacksmith shop, farm equipment and livestock. Twenty-five pioneering pilgrims arrived in 1823. Due to the paucity of investors and settlers, the colony foundered, and the buildings were burned to the ground in 1836 during the Second Seminole War. The colony had survived thirteen years. Moses Elias Levy died in 1854. Although his son would become an ardent defender of slavery, Moses Levy remained a lifelong abolitionist having published in London in 1823 a treatise outlining his plan for the abolition of slavery.[29] Unfortunately, no trace of **Pilgrimage Plantation** remains today.

After working on his father's plantation and familiarizing himself with Florida, which became a territory of United States in 1821, after the sparsely-populated state was ceded by Spain, David Levy moved to **Saint Augustine, to** study law. He was admitted to the Florida bar in 1832 and elected to the territorial Legislative Council in 1836. From 1841 to 1845 he served as a delegate to the U.S.

---

[29] Levy, Moses E., *A Plan for the Abolition of Slavery, Consistently with the Interests of All Parties Concerned*, edited by Chris Monaco, Micanopy, Fl., The Wacahoota Press, 1999.

House of Representatives from the Florida Territory. An active proponent of statehood, his efforts were rewarded when Florida was admitted to the union as the 27th state in 1845, despite strong opposition from many Floridians who wanted to postpone statehood until the territory accumulated a large enough population to create two states with the Apalachicola and Chattahoochee Rivers as the boundary between East Florida and West Florida. Given the state of Florida politics in the twenty-first century, the two-state plan was perhaps not such a bad idea!

Thirty-five years previously, British and American settlers in the western part of Spanish West Florida between the Mississippi and Pearl rivers, styling themselves "patriots" and encouraged by the United States, fomented an armed insurrection, sequestered the Spanish governor, Don Carlos de Hault de Lassus, and established the Republic of West Florida on September 23, 1810, with St. Francisville as its capital. Their flag, a single white star on a blue background, was later known as the "Bonnie Blue." The ephemeral "republic" was annexed by the United States under President James Madison less than three months later, on December 6, 1810, and now comprises the eight Florida parishes of eastern Louisiana. Don Carlos was subsequently court-marshaled by the Spanish and sentenced to death, but the sentence was never executed.

This procedure of American settlers occupying foreign territory, complaining about the lack of freedom under a tyrannical yoke, followed by a declaration of independence and an appeal for annexation by the United States, was the dress rehearsal for similar scenarios that would be enacted in Texas in 1836, California in 1846 and Hawaii in 1894.

Until the Seventeenth Amendment was enacted in 1917, senators were chosen by the legislatures in their states. Accordingly, David Levy was elected to represent Florida in the United States Senate and sworn in on July 1, 1845, making him the first Jewish senator in American history.

In 1845, the Florida legislature officially allowed David Levy to change his last name to "Yulee," the Americanized spelling of his grandfather's Sephardic avonymic. The following year, he married a devout Presbyterian, Nannie Christian Wickliffe, the daughter of Charles A. Wickliffe, who first served as the Governor of Kentucky, then Postmaster General of the United States before his election to the House of Representatives in 1861. The couple had four children.

After his defeat for reëlection in 1850, David Yulee set out to realize his dream of constructing a railroad straight across the wilderness of the Florida peninsula to link the deep-water ports of Fernandina, on Amelia Island on the Atlantic, and Cedar Key, on the Gulf of Mexico, via Gainesville. Work began in 1853. According to Eliot Kleinberg, "Building conditions were brutal; the first 10 miles of the 155-mile line took nearly a year."[30] Today, State Route 200, U.S. Route 301 and State Route 24 trace David Yulee's Florida Railroad line. The first train arrived in Cedar Key on March 1, 1861; the War Between the States broke out six weeks later. Yulee thereupon resigned from the Senate and returned to Florida to continue operating his plantation, Marguerita, hidden in the dense woods bordering the Homosassa River north of Tampa. Yulee was a reluctant supporter of the Confederacy, but supplied its armies with citrus fruits, cotton and sugar from his plantation. The sugar mill operated from 1851 to May 29, 1864, when Union troops burned the plantation buildings to the ground. Yulee was at his second home near Gainesville during the attack and avoided capture.

After the War, Yulee, whose pro-slavery rhetoric in the Senate had earned him the sobriquet of "Florida Fire-Eater," was taken into custody at Gainesville and convicted of treason. After being imprisoned in Fort Pulaski, Georgia, for nine months, he was pardoned by President Andrew Johnson in 1866.

David Yulee promptly set about rebuilding his trans-Florida railroad, which had been devastated during the War: the Union had blockaded the seaports and the Confederacy had requisitioned the tracks. In 1870, a depot was built in the hamlet of Rosewood, a predominantly African-American

---

[30] Kleinberg, Eliot, *Historical Traveler's Guide to Florida.* Sarasota: Pineapple Press, Inc., 2006.

community which would be destroyed and abandoned as a consequence of the infamous Rosewood Massacre of January 1, 1923.

David Yulee later served as president of three other railroad companies that failed and were liquidated: the Peninsular Railroad Company, the Tropical Florida Railway Company and the Fernandina and Jacksonville Railroad Company. Unpaid investors sued Yulee, and one case, Yulee v. Rose, went to the United States Supreme Court.

After the demise of his railroads, David Yulee and his wife retired to Washington, DC, in 1881, where they commissioned a residence at 1305 Connecticut Avenue, NW, just south of Dupont Circle. Designed by the architect Charles H. Reed Jr., the Yulee Mansion cost $40,000. It was razed in 1916 to permit the construction of an apartment building.

David Levy Yulee died of pneumonia while on a trip to New York on October 10, 1886, and was buried in Oak Hill Cemetery in Washington's Georgetown neighborhood. The town of Yulee, Florida, and Levy County, Florida, are named for him, and the ruins of his sugar plantation have been preserved as the Yulee Sugar Mill Ruins Historic State Park in Homosassa. Since 1995, the city of Archer, Florida, has celebrated an annual Yulee Railroad Day in early June, and in 2000 David Levy Yulee was declared a Great Floridian by the Florida Department of State.

Judah Philip Benjamin (1811-1884)

Judah P. Benjamin was born on August 11, 1811, in Christiansted, on the island of Saint Croix, also in the Danish West Indies.[31] His parents, Philip Benjamin and the former Rebecca de Mendes, were Sephardic Jews who had been shopkeepers in London and emigrated while the islands were still under British occupation. Consequently, both Judah P. Benjamin and David Levy acquired British nationality at their birth. Judah's mother's family had been prominent in Spain before the expulsion of Jews in 1492 during the regime of King Ferdinand and Queen Isabel, *Los Reyes Católicos*. In 1822, the family emigrated to America, settling in Charleston, South Carolina, "the nation's most Jewish city" at the time. By 1800, Charleston had more Jews than any other city in North America. Nell Porter Brown reported in the *Harvard Magazine* that a document drafted in 1669 by the philosopher John Locke granted the right of people

---

[31] In his correspondence to his sister, Peninah Kruttschnitt, Benjamin gives his birthday as August 6 and states that he spent his childhood on Saint Thomas.

of any religion except Catholics to form a church in South Carolina, opening the door not only for Jews but for French Huguenots.[32]

Benjamin enrolled at Yale in 1825 at the age of 14 and was a top student until he left abruptly in 1827 for "ungentlemanly conduct," which remains unelucidated. The young Judah promptly headed for New Orleans where, according to Rabbi Bertram Wallace Korn in *The Early Jews of New Orleans*, he "arrived in 1828 with no visible assets other than wit, charm, [an] omnivorous mind and boundless energy." Eager to pass the Louisiana bar, requiring fluency in both French and English, Judah found employment tutoring English to Mademoiselle Natalie Beauché de Saint-Martin, the 16-year old daughter of French colonial aristocrats who had fled the Haitian slave revolt of 1791. Natalie perfected her English and Judah became proficient in French. They were married in 1833. Judah did not renounce his faith, but agreed that any children would be raised Catholic; in 1843 Natalie gave birth to their only child, Anne Julie Marie Natalie, nicknamed Ninette.

Admitted to the Louisiana bar in 1832 at the age of 21, he promptly developed a flourishing law practice that enabled him to offer Natalie a four-story Greek Revival townhouse at 327 Bourbon Street in the Vieux Carré of New Orleans in 1835,

---

[32] Brown, Nell Porter, "A Portion of the People," in *Harvard Magazine*, January-February 2003.

and the Bellechasse sugar plantation downstream in Plaquemines Parish. A member of the Whig Party, he was elected to the Louisiana House of Representatives in 1842. Because of his frequent absences and because of Natalie's frivolous and promiscuous nature, the marriage was strained and Natalie separated from her husband, took Ninette and departed for Paris in 1845. After a brief trip to Washington in 1852, where she was beleaguered by scandalous rumors surrounding her conduct, she returned to Paris for the remainder of her life. Benjamin would thereafter voyage each summer to Paris to visit Natalie and Ninette. Since he no longer had the time to manage Bellechasse and since Natalie was in Paris, he sold the plantation and granted manumission to his slaves, numbering more than a hundred, in 1850.[33]

The Louisiana State Legislature elected Judah P. Benjamin to the Senate in 1852, but upon his arrival in Washington he was promptly offered a position as a justice of the Supreme Court by President Millard Fillmore. The *New York Times* commented that, "If the President nominates Benjamin, the Democrats are determined to confirm him." Benjamin declined the president's offer in order to serve in the Senate, thereby missing the chance to become the first Jewish justice of the Supreme

---

[33] "Judah P. Benjamin and Slavery," a thorough study of Benjamin's complex and ambiguous views on the subject by Maury Wiseman, was published in *The American Jewish Archives Journal*, Vol 59, No. 1 & 2 (2007).

Court.[34] He also declined an appointment as ambassador to Spain in 1853 and another nomination to the Supreme Court, by Fillmore's successor, Franklin Pierce, in 1854.

Shortly after swearing the oath of office on March 4, 1853, Judah P. Benjamin challenged another freshman senator, Jefferson F. Davis of Mississippi, to a duel following an altercation over a perceived insult. Davis apologized and he and Benjamin developed a close political alliance that would endure over many decades.

Benjamin acquired a reputation as an eloquent orator who defended the doctrine of states' rights based primarily on the Tenth Amendment to the Constitution—that the Union was a compact of sovereign states from which any could secede. As a Jewish defender of slavery, he was assailed during a debate on the floor of the Senate by the abolitionist Benjamin Franklin "Bluff" Wade[35] of Ohio, who accused him of being "an Israelite with Egyptian principles." Benjamin is reported to have responded, "It is true that I am a Jew, and when my ancestors were receiving their Ten Commandments from the immediate Deity, amidst the thunderings and lightnings of Mount Sinai, the ancestors of my

---

[34] That honor fell to Louis Brandeis, appointed by President Woodrow Wilson in 1916.

[35] Had the impeachment of Andrew Johnson in 1868 led to a conviction at trial in the Senate, Wade would have assumed the presidential powers and duties.

opponent were herding swine in the forests of Britain."

Judah P. Benjamin was reëlected to the Senate in 1858, but following the election of Abraham Lincoln as president in 1860, he realized that secession was inevitable and decided to resign his Senate seat. His farewell address, delivered on December 31, 1860, before a crowded Senate Gallery, was described by his biographer, Eli N. Evans,[36] as "one of the great speeches in American history."

Benjamin formally resigned from the Senate on February 4, 1861, and received an appointment as Attorney General of the Confederate States of America on February 25. President Jefferson Davis recognized his high reputation as a lawyer and "the lucidity of his intellect, his systematic habits and his capacity for labor." According to Evans, following the first cabinet meeting, Secretary of War Leroy P. Walker declared "There was only one man there who had any sense, and that man was Benjamin."

Benjamin later replaced Walker as Secretary of War, shouldering the blame for many shortcomings suffered by the Confederate armies and engaging in publicized quarrels with Generals P. G. T. Beauregard and Thomas "Stonewall" Jackson. Following popular anger and a censure by the

---

[36] Evans, Eli N., *Judah P. Benjamin – The Jewish Confederate*. New York, Free Press, 1988.

Confederate Congress, he resigned his position and in March 1862 was appointed Secretary of State, where he served as Jefferson Davis's close associate until the conclusion of hostilities. Benjamin's primary goal was to secure diplomatic recognition of the Confederacy by Great Britain and France. These efforts were unsuccessful, so he convinced Jefferson Davis of the necessity of developing other means to import the supplies vitally needed for the survival of the Confederacy. Benjamin dispatched agents to Bermuda, the West Indies and Cuba to implement this project. Almost forty percent of the blockade runners were steamships specially constructed in the shipyards of the Firth of Clyde in Scotland and designed with low silhouettes, light draft and high speed enabling them to cruise undetected. With the introduction of blockade running, Benjamin's reputation recovered, and his esteem by Jefferson Davis reached its apogee when he was depicted on the two-dollar Confederate banknote issued in 1864.

On to Florida! With the end of the war in sight, Jefferson Davis and his cabinet were compelled to evacuate Richmond, the Confederate capital, by train, on April 2, 1865. They reached Danville, Virginia, where they remained for a week before heading for the Carolinas. General Robert E. Lee's surrender to General Ulysses S. Grant at Appomattox Courthouse, Virginia, followed on April 9, 1865, and Benjamin and the other Confederate cabinet members became wanted men. The Confederate Secret Service had set up a spy ring in Canada and Benjamin had transferred between half a million and a million dollars in gold to Canadian banks to finance these operations. One of his agents was John H. Surratt Jr., who served as a courier, moving messages and contraband across Union lines. Surratt was involved in a scheme to kidnap President Lincoln, and he and his mother, Mary, were implicated in the plot to assassinate the President. Benjamin's connection to Surratt brought him under suspicion—never proved—that he had participated in the conspiracy. [37]

The party continued south. Whereas most of the Confederates remained silent and dejected, Benjamin was light-hearted, reciting from memory verse after verse of Tennyson's *Ode on the Death of the Duke of Wellington* to uplift their spirits. When the fugitives reached Abbeville, South Carolina, on May 2, he left the party, proposing to join President Davis in Texas, where it was believed Confederate forces were still holding their ground. Jefferson Davis would be captured on May 10, 1865, near Irwinville, Georgia, but a wagon train under armed guard, bearing official documents and, some believe, gold specie and bullion, succeeded in reaching David Yulee's Cotton Wood Plantation in Archer, Florida, on May 22, 1865, where the contents were dispersed and concealed.

---

[37] Mary Surratt owned an inn in Washington, DC, where the plotters boarded. After being tried and convicted, she and three others were hanged on July 7, 1865. Historians are still divided on her culpability or innocence. John Surratt was released after a mistrial.

In what the *New York Times* of August 3, 1865, described as a "mythical escape," Benjamin continued south incognito, employing various disguises and pseudonyms. Because he spoke fluent French, he escaped capture by posing as a Monsieur Bonfals, a French journalist who spoke no English and was accompanied by a former Confederate officer who pretended to be his interpreter. On May 1, 1865, Federal agents had intensified their efforts to locate all Confederate fugitives. With a $40,000 dead-or-alive bounty on his head, and Union forces hot on his trail, Benjamin employed another disguise, pretending to be a South Carolinian farmer and cattle trader named Charles Howard. On two occasions, as Federal troops approached, he sought refuge in a canebrake. He finally reached Monticello, Florida, not far from the Georgia border, on May 13, before moving on to Tampa and then Ellenton, where he was offered aid and succor by Captain Archibald McNeill in the Gamble Mansion on the banks of the Manatee River estuary. Captain McNeill owned a fleet of blockade-running sloops and schooners that transported goods in and out South Florida at night, sailing silently and furtively along islands and inlets to avoid detection by the Federal Navy blockading Confederate ports and seaways.

In a letter he wrote to his younger sister Peninah Kruttschnitt from Nassau on July 22, 1865, Benjamin recounts the details of his harrowing escape by sea. After spending close to a month in the Gamble Mansion recovering from his ordeal and intent on reaching England, he crossed the Manatee, procured a small yawl and hired two "trusty persons" to accompany him, Captain Frederic Tresca, a former blockade runner of French nationality, and Hiram A. McLeod, an experienced sailor. The trio set out from Bradenton on June 23 and endured frequent squalls and lack of sleep on the six-hundred-mile journey down the west coast of the Florida peninsula, reaching Knight's Key around July 7. There, they boarded a larger boat, the *Blonde*, and traversed the Straits of Florida encountering more squalls, water-spouts and tropical storms before arriving on Bimini, in the Bahamas, on the tenth of July. Three days later, he transferred to a sloop transporting a cargo of sponges to Nassau, but the following morning the sloop foundered, sinking with such rapidity that Benjamin had barely time to jump into a small skiff that the sloop had in tow, along with "three Negroes for my companions in disaster." With no provisions other than a pot of rice and a small keg of water and only one oar, the shipwrecked quartet were finally rescued by the crew of the Light House Yacht *Georgina*, "a fine large brig," and were returned to Bimini on Saturday, June 15. Benjamin met Tresca and McLeod, and paid Tresca for his passage with $1,000 in gold coins he had sewn inside his clothing, reimbursed Tresca's and McLeod's expenses and sent presents to Tresca's wife and Mrs. McNeil.

Thwarted in his first attempt, Benjamin immediately chartered another sloop and set sail once more from Bimini to Nassau. Although the distance was only a hundred miles, calms, storms and headwinds so delayed their progress that they reached their destination after six days. He then left Nassau for Havana on the morning of July 22, arriving on the twenty-fifth, "after a very favorable passage." He wrote to Peninah from Havana on the first of August and departed for England, via Saint Thomas, by steamer on August 6, which he declared to be his birthday.

In a subsequent letter to Peninah, written from "17 Savile Row, London," on September 29, 1865, Benjamin continued the narrative of his adventures. As the small ship he had taken from Havana approached Saint Thomas, a fire broke out in the hold, but the crew succeeded in extinguishing the flames and the ship managed to reach its destination "with seven feet of water in the hold...and the deck burned to within an eighth of an inch of the entire thickness." While awaiting the steamer that would take him to England, Benjamin took advantage of his stay on the island to visit the scenes of his early childhood, although his memory was "very indistinct, as I was a mere infant when we left that island for Wilmington [North Carolina]." On August 13, Benjamin set out from Saint Thomas on the final leg of his voyage and arrived at Southampton on August 30, 1865, after a perilous odyssey of almost five months. [38]

---

[38] Sources for the account of Benjamin's escape are *Judah P. Benjamin* by Pierce Butler and *Judah P. Benjamin: Confederate Statesman*, by Robert Douthat Meade.

In England, Benjamin, found himself once again without liquid assets and, having burned all his personal papers and records before leaving Richmond, reinvented himself and began life anew. He was admitted to the British bar in June 1866 and commenced a law career, becoming an influential and prosperous barrister. In 1868, he published *Benjamin's Treatise on the Law of Sale of Personal Property,* known as "Benjamin on Sales," that became a classic in Britain and America. It was published in three editions during his lifetime; an eighth edition was published as recently as 2010. Benjamin also became closer to his wife, offering her a grand *hôtel particulier* at 41, Avenue d'Iéna, in Paris. He sponsored and organized Ninette's lavish nuptials to Captain Henri de Boursignac, celebrated in the church of Saint Pierre de Chaillot on September 7, 1874, and settled on her a dowry of $3,000 a year. In March 1875 he wrote that his new son-in-law was "all that I could desire."

When he retired in 1883 for reasons of ill health, Benjamin crossed the Channel to Paris to join his wife, his daughter and his grandchildren. He died on May 6, 1884, from a fall from his carriage, at the age of 72. Although he had never renounced his faith, he was buried under the Frenchified name of Philippe Benjamin in the Père Lachaise cemetery in the crypt of the Boursignac family, his daughter's Catholic in-laws. It was not until 1938 that the United Daughters of the Confederacy placed a plaque on his grave identifying him properly. His three grandchildren died in childhood and no direct descendants have survived. Natalie died in 1891,

Ninette died in 1898 and the Bellechasse Plantation was demolished in March 1960.

Daniel Brook reports in an article published in the online magazine *Tablet* in 2012[39] that Benjamin's townhouse in New Orleans was converted in modern times into a strip club known as Temptations; one of its ecdysiasts, "Ryan" Lockhart, confided to Brook that the upper floors are haunted by Ninette's ghost "searching for her absentee father." The Gamble Mansion is now the centerpiece of the Judah P. Benjamin Confederate Memorial at Gamble Plantation Historic State Park and is open to the public.

*****

In some ways, Moses Elias Levy was more fascinating than his son. An ardent and articulate abolitionist and egalitarian, his fervent opposition to slavery resulted in a rupture with his son that was never healed: the two never reconciled. Always a progressive thinker, but also deeply religious, he decided to invest his fortune in a charitable cause by realizing his vision, Pilgrimage Plantation. As 20-term Congressman Henry Waxman observed in an interview in 2009, "Jewish values place a great emphasis on compassion and trying to help other people, and the doctrine of *tikkun olam*, trying to repair the world." Moses Levy's dream was realized to a certain extent because today Florida has the

---

[39] Brook, Daniel, "The Forgotten Confederate Jew," in *Tablet*, July 17, 2012.

third largest population of Jews of any state in the Union.

David Levy Yulee, like his father, was a visionary but, in his case, the future lay in transportation. He became known as the Father of Florida Railroads and his trans-peninsular Florida Railroad certainly inspired William Flagler, who launched construction of the Florida East Cost Railway a half-century later.

Judah P. Benjamin rendered his multifaceted and enigmatic life difficult for historians and thwarted their research by burning all his archives and personal papers. Pierce Butler, in the preface to his biography of Benjamin published in 1907, cites a conversation between Benjamin and Francis Lawley, an earlier biographer, on April 27, 1883, in which Benjamin stated, "No letters addressed to me by others will be found among my papers when I die...I have read so many American biographies which reflected only the passions and prejudices of their writers, that I do not want to leave behind my letters and documents to be used in such a work about myself."

Although some characterized him as the South's "dark prince," most historians concur with the sentiment that Judah P. Benjamin was "the brains of the Confederacy."

Frolicking on the Beach with John

This is a friend's Real Story.

I.

Life is what happens when you're making other plans.
John Lennon

Call me Cassandra. Like my namesake from Greek mythology, people often disbelieve me. I spent most of my professional life in Nashville, where I taught underprivileged first-graders to read. I applied for and received a Fulbright Scholarship to study in the United Kingdom. Upon my return, I began applying a methodology inspired by Benjamin Bloom's taxonomy of thinking skills, with surprisingly successful results.

When I retired, I moved to Palm Beach County and became a Floridian. I lived for twelve years on Palm Beach Island, where I worked in a shop on Worth Avenue in what is known as the Gucci Courtyard and became acquainted with hundreds of customers among the rich and not-so-rich, many of whom are still my friends.

In late June 1979, having divorced my husband, I took my daughter, Melissa, age fourteen, to Spain where we planned to spend the summer. After arriving in Málaga on the Costa del Sol, I rented an automobile. We drove south to Marbella and continued to nearby Puerto Banús, where we found accommodations in a hotel and planned to use it as our base. The town was founded by Juan Banús, a prominent Madrileño property developer, who named it after himself.

Frequented by movie stars, royalty and millionaires, the resort has gained a place alongside Monte Carlo, St. Tropez, Sanremo and Porto Cervo as a playground of the rich and famous and a place to see and be seen along the shores of the Mediterranean. The marina at Puerto Banús accommodates many yachts, but some of the superyachts are so large that they need to be anchored offshore and passengers and crew ferried ashore by helicopter.

When we checked in at the hotel, I couldn't find the book of traveler's checks I had purchased in America. I had no idea whatsoever of when or where or how I had lost them, but this didn't present a problem since the checks would be replaced in due course.

Everywhere I travel, if there's a beach, that's where I want to go first. After checking in to the hotel, Melissa and I changed into our swimwear and made a beeline for the Mediterranean. She was still annoyed at the loss of our traveler's checks and was loudly berating me for my carelessness: "Mother, I can't believe this! We've only been in Spain two days, and you've already lost all our traveler's checks!" At that moment, a man who looked to be in his late thirties, wearing a Greek fisherman's cap and round, wire-rimmed glasses with tinted lenses, accompanied by an adolescent boy who appeared to be around Melissa's age, approached us from the opposite direction. Both were pale; they certainly hadn't been in the area long enough to acquire a suntan.

"Is there a problem?" the stranger inquired.

"My mother lost all our traveler's checks," my daughter blurted.

"Perhaps I can help," he answered, withdrawing a fat roll of money out of his pocket and peeling off several hundred-dollar bills. I noticed that the wristwatch he was wearing had sparkles on it—were they diamonds?

"We can't take your money," I explained, "The traveler's checks will be replaced."

"Well, at least will you accept my invitation for dinner with my son and me tonight?"

Before I could say anything, Melissa, who was making eyes at the young man, announced peremptorily "Yes!" before I could veto the proposal.

"Then, it's settled. Let's meet for drinks in the Sinatra Bar at 7:30 tonight." The Sinatra Bar is the most famous watering hole in Puerto Banús, an excellent observation post where hoi polloi can play spot-the-celebrity and ogle the yachts in the marina and the Ferraris and Lamborghinis as they slink by, grumbling in low gear.

The four of us spent the remainder of the afternoon frolicking on the beach. At one point, we came across a man with a donkey cart loaded with bottles of beer on ice. My new friend snatched a bottle from the cart, popped the cap and swigged it there and then. He peppered his speech with puns and word play; having lived in England, I thought I recognized a Liverpudlian accent, but we were all having such a good time that I didn't think much about it. I also noticed what appeared to be a few paparazzi lurking at a distance.

When we came to a huge yacht with a wooden hull, my newfound friend jumped aboard and importuned me to join him. I politely refused since I had no idea whether this friendly stranger was the owner or not, and was not eager to be arrested for trespassing, especially since I had no funds aside from a few pesetas in my purse.

Melissa and I returned to the hotel to dress for dinner. They used the European system where guests entrust their room key at the reception desk when leaving and pick it up upon their return. When I asked for our key, the desk clerk asked me how I had got to know John Lennon: "You were seen walking on the beach with John Lennon this afternoon." "What? I didn't know it was John

Lennon!" My incredulity must have added to my naïveté and made me appear even more of a fool.

We met for drinks and dinner as scheduled. But my new friend wasn't satisfied with the wines on the list. He knew exactly what he wanted and seemed to be on intimate terms with the wine steward, who accompanied him downstairs into the private wine cellar where he selected a bottle of one of his favorite vintages. John and Julian apparently enjoyed our company, too, because Melissa and I were invited to board their yacht for a cruise to Monte Carlo! Knowing that he was married at the time, I succeeded in declining his invitation before Melissa impetuously accepted it.

After Lennon and his son left Puerto Banús, Melissa and I became *les célébrités du jour*. A photographer who went by the name of Rafaél shot portraits of us with his Hasselblad. I started receiving invitations to the swanky Marbella Club from total strangers who had learned about the "mystery lady" accompanying John Lennon on the beach. One of them even offered to buy me a condo!

II.

*If everyone demanded peace
instead of another television set,
then there'd be peace.*
John Lennon

In the autumn of 2007, Melissa and I returned to Europe, intending to spend a holiday in Marbella. We took advantage of our stay to search for

177

photographs documenting our encounter with John Lennon and Julian, because after we had returned to the United States in 1979, friends had told us that photographs of Lennon with "some unidentified people" on the Costa del Sol had been published in the newspapers. We contacted the editor of the local English-language journal, who helped us search the publication's photographic archives. We found a file labeled "Lennon" but, surprisingly, it was empty. The contents had been expunged. The editor also informed us that Rafaél, the photographer who had taken pictures of Melissa and me, had died in an automobile accident.

III.

The more I see the less I know for sure.
John Lennon

My friend Ronald, the author of this book, tells me that he consulted six biographies of John Lennon in the Mandel Public Library in West Palm Beach, including Tim Riley's 765-page *Lennon: The Man, the Myth, the Music* and the 851-page *John Lennon: The Life*, by Philip Norman. He could find no mention of John Lennon and his son Julian sailing on a yacht along the Costa del Sol in the summer of 1979. None of these biographies mentions anything happening in the life of John Lennon in the month of June 1979: it's a complete blank, a *tabula rasa*.

Ronald told me that the closest event he found to June 1979 in the chronology of John Lennon's life was a reference in Philip Norman's book to a

178

birthday party thrown for Julian—born April 8, 1963—celebrated at El Solano, a nine-bedroom mansion on Palm Beach Island, of all places! Ronald would say that John Lennon had become a Floridian, too, albeit briefly. Lennon had purchased El Solano from Mildred "Brownie" McLean for $725,000. Overlooking the Atlantic at 720 South Ocean Boulevard, the Mediterranean Revival building was designed by the legendary Palm Beach architect Addison Mizner and built in 1925. I am told that, after passing through the hands of a number of owners, El Solano was sold for $23 million in January 2016.

IV.

Reality leaves a lot to the imagination.
John Lennon

That is the end of my friend's story. In June 1980, John Lennon rented a 43-foot sloop, the *Megan Jaye*, and sailed the 700 miles from Newport, Rhode Island, to St. George's, Bermuda, with a crew of four. During the two months he spent on the island, calling himself John Greene, he began composing the music for *Double Fantasy*, the last studio album released during his lifetime, and *Milk and Honey*, released posthumously. He returned to New York, where he was murdered on December 8, 1980, at the age of forty, three weeks after the release of *Double Fantasy*. A photograph taken the morning of his death by Paul Goresh shows him wearing his characteristic Greek fisherman's cap and tinted glasses.

What do *you* think John Lennon was doing in June 1979?

Index

182

185

About the Author

Writer-photographer-lecturer Ronald W. Kenyon was born and raised in Ashland, Kentucky. He was admitted to the Honors Program at the University of Michigan, Ann Arbor, where he specialized in English, political science, French and Spanish and won two Hopwood writing awards. The recipient of a Woodrow Wilson National Fellowship, he attended graduate school at Stanford University. He also studied at Saint Lawrence University under a National Defense Education Act scholarship.

Ronald W. Kenyon spent over thirty years living and working in France and the Middle East and has visited 48 countries in the Americas, Europe, Asia and Africa. Although nominally retired, Ronald W. Kenyon continues his writing and photography: projects in both areas are in progress. Like most of the characters in this book, he is a transplanted Floridian.

Ronald W. Kenyon is a member of Artists of Palm Beach County.

Also by Ronald W. Kenyon

Divagations: Collected Poetry 1959-1996
A Winter in the Middle of Two Seas: Real Stories from Bahrain
Monville: Forgotten Luminary of the French Enlightenment
Monville: l'inconnu des Lumières (en français)
Le Petit Kenyon: Dining in the Environs of Paris for Walkers
Statues of Liberty: Real Stories from France
On the Trail in France

Photography

Metro Portraits
Metro Messages
My Beautiful France: Landscapes
Ile-de-France, terres d'inspiration (en français)
France Images & Messages

187

188

November 21, 2016
39295

189

Made in the USA
Columbia, SC
21 May 2020